Embroidery in Miniature

Jean Brown

Embroidery in Miniature

B.T. Batsford Ltd · London

ISBN 0 7134 5438 5

Typeset by Servis Filmsetting Ltd, Manchester
and printed in Great Britain by
Anchor Brendon Ltd
Tiptree, Essex
for the publishers
B.T. Batsford Ltd
4 Fitzhardinge Street
London W1H 0AH

To my family who cheerfully allowed me to become an embroiderer and an author, and most particularly to my mother, May Plummer, whose skill and encouragement have provided me with inspiration through the years, and many samples for this book.

Contents

Acknowledgements   9

1 Introduction   11

2 Materials   18

3 Inspiration for design   27

4 Basic priorities for design in miniature   31

5 Experiments in design   37

6 Preparation for the embroidery   58

7 Techniques   60

8 Construction   97

9 Finishing and framing   102

10 Larger embroideries incorporating
   miniature techniques   112

   Suppliers   116

   Book list   118

   Index   120

Acknowledgements

It would be impossible to name all the people who, over the years, have taught me so much about embroidery. For this book, also, I have been helped and encouraged by the generosity of fellow embroiderers in lending their work, and many are mentioned in the photograph captions. Others have contributed valuable ideas on specific techniques or allowed me to photograph work from their own collections. These include Val Anderson, Peggy Bailey, Sue Barlow, Carol Black, Dawn Lockyer, Elizabeth Parker, Vivienne Stubbs, Hannah Taylor and Sheila Yates.

I would also like to thank in particular all the members of the South Birmingham Branch of the Embroiderers' Guild, contributing work and ideas, and cheerfully accepting that their chairman was obsessed with miniature embroidery.

I am grateful to Sheila Phipps, and the Burrell Collection, Glasgow Museums and Art Galleries for advice and photographs of work in the collection.

All the photographs in the book (unless otherwise stated) were taken by Neville Roberts and Crom Waldron who were assisted by Mary Roberts and Lily Waldron. I thank them for their patience and professionalism. My thanks also to my daughter, Sarah Williams-Brown, for producing all the necessary enlargements.

Rachel Wright, of Batsford, gave me the initial encouragement for the project and has been helpful through every process of production.

Note

All drawings and embroidery are the work of the author, unless otherwise stated. In some photographs a £1 coin has been included to give a scale size. This coin is 2.3 cm in diameter ($\frac{7}{8}$ in.).

1 Introduction

The fascination of miniature items and workmanship is not confined to the world of children. Like them we marvel at what has been intricately made, finding great pleasure in those things that we can hold in the palm of our hand. All the world's great civilisations have produced tiny artefacts varying in materials and purpose, from jewellery to objects placed in graves as part of a religious ceremonial. The 'toys' of earlier centuries in our own society were often collectors' pieces, sought by adults rather than the playthings of childen. In recent years interest has revived in the world of the miniature. Collecting and making model railways, small scale soldiers, boats and aeroplanes has always been very popular. Now the doll and the dollshouse have come back into their own again as items which can be collected and admired by adults. The workmanship that is necessary for their making has been given the credit it deserves.

Hopefully we have discarded a narrow view of embroidery where only useful items with some added decoration are considered worthy of the time spent upon them. With the recent growth of interest in embroidery miniature items are often the subject of exhibitions and competitions. It is perhaps our lack of time and space that makes us value such small pieces, and a growing awareness of the cost of materials and labour encourages this interest. Small gifts, embroidery for costume, jewellery, dolls and dollshouses can be worked in a variety of techniques and fabrics. The design and skill involved is not of a different order to any other type of embroidery, but it is based upon a different perspective. This book aims to encourage embroiderers to look at design material, at fabrics, threads and techniques and see the many possibilities. Hopefully readers will also explore more ideas – one of the joys of communicating one's own enthusiasm is that there is no end to that exploration. Each of us contributes our individuality to the threads of history.

The aims of this book

A definition of 'embroidery in miniature' obviously has to be discussed in an introduction to the subject. Embroidery is no longer restricted to just stitchery, and many exhibitions feature embroidery combined with weaving, knitting, paper, etc. Here, basically, techniques are presented involving the use of fabric, thread and needle – however, widely construed that may be.

In exhibitions and competitions a limit of about 15 cm (6 in.) in any dimension is often given as the maximum size, and this provides an interesting challenge in combining good design and an appropriate technique. Thus, most of the work shown in this book is about this size and under. There are occasions, however, when examples of miniature embroidery can be included in much larger pieces – some such examples have been included as they demonstrate similar principles.

The list of articles in which miniature embroidery is an integral part can be a long one, but it shows the great variety open to embroiderers with many varying interests. The possibilities include – jewellery, dolls clothes and accessories, dollshouse textiles; mobiles, small soft sculptures, advent calendars; fans, small bags and purses; paper weights, pin cushions; cases for needles, spectacles, scissors, notepads; covers for small books; decorated lids for boxes; small complete boxes; children's toys and 'executive toys'; greetings cards and framed pictures; bookmarks.

One of the distinct advantages of working in miniature is that each piece can be embroidered on a small frame or without any frame at all and carried around easily, making it ideal for holidays and leisure time. Lengthy train journeys and interminable committee meetings have been made more pleasurable for me this way, and it is always intriguing to see how many people take an interest in the embroidery.

Although some of the examples in this book have been worked for a specific purpose such as a needle case or a dollshouse carpet or greetings card, many of the samples have been deliberately left unmounted. Much of the embroidery shown and the techniques described could be adapted for a variety of articles, and I hope that this gives a wider perspective on what can be attempted and achieved.

While preparing this book I have come into contact with many skilled embroiderers, of all levels of experience and with many varied interests who are creating beautiful miniature pieces. It would not be possible to show all their work or even acknowledge the names of those I have met and have been told about. Yet I hope that they will realize that they have given inspiration and great satisfaction to those of us who see their work. I have tried to include as many examples as possible to show the different facets of miniature embroidery and the skill of those embroiderers who find a particular fascination in the craft.

A brief history of miniature embroidery

There are two ways of looking at miniature embroidery when we delve into the history of techniques and the artefacts of previous generations. We can be greatly inspired by the fine detail that is found in so much earlier work spanning the world, from the stitchery of China to the metal thread of underside couching in Britain, and across the centuries as well. Look again at examples of work which depend on very fine threads, needles and a complementary backing material. There are many kinds of stitches which have been used in this way, and techniques have been adapted to suit the particular demands of the item that is being made. Yet perhaps of more relevance here are the miniature pieces of embroidery that can be found in museums and private collections.

The popularity of canvas work across the centuries and its versatility has meant that many miniature articles have been produced. Two illustrations here show how fine detail has been

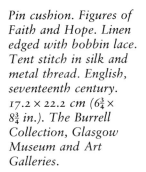

Pin cushion. Figures of Faith and Hope. Linen edged with bobbin lace. Tent stitch in silk and metal thread. English, seventeenth century. 17.2 × 22.2 cm (6¾ × 8¾ in.). The Burrell Collection, Glasgow Museum and Art Galleries.

Compact case lid. Pastoral landscape. Tent stitch in silk on fine canvas (approximately 45 threads to 2.5 cm (1 in.). Austrian, early twentieth century. 7 cm (2¾ in.) square.

part of that tradition in different countries and eras. The pin cushion is an English example from the seventeenth century and was worked in silk and metal thread. It shows the figures of Faith and Hope, and was embroidered in tent stitch. The left hand figure has the arm and face worked in a split stitch and the three dimensional detail of the beads around the neck is particularly attractive. The other illustration is of an item from Austria dating from this century. It was found in a jumble sale and appears to be the top of a powder compact or mirror case. There are approximately 18 threads to the centimetre (45 threads to the inch) on the canvas used. Apparently, such fine work was still being done in Austria in the 1950s. The Victorians however, must have worked more threads into canvas than people in any other era, and many examples can be found of useful objects and decorative articles made from all kinds of material from Berlin wool to beads. The durability of embroidery on canvas has meant that there are still surviving examples and also explains its modern popularity for items such as needle and spectacle cases.

The seventeenth century in Britain was the time when the fashion for three dimensional embroidery was developed into a high art, with boxes embellished with fine needlelace and stump work techniques. Although these boxes are much too large to discuss here, they contain many superlative details of figures,

Flower spray. Silk, gold and leather. English circa 1700. 17.8 cm (7 in.) long. The Burrell Collection, Glasgow Museums and Art Galleries.

Fragment from bedhanging. Linen and muslin, with flower in chain stitch, quilting in back stitch. English late seventeenth century. 15 × 10 cm (6 × 4 in.). Private collection.

trees, and buildings which are basically miniature embroideries. The illustration above dates from around 1700 and show such three dimensional techniques taken to what we would now call 'soft sculpture'. The flower spray is made of wire, silk, gold thread and leather and is possibly English.

I chose the illustration of the flower because, although it comes from a bed hanging, it is a delightful small design in itself. The flower and leaf motif are worked in a shaded range of colours in fine chain stitch. The quilting pattern is in back stitch and would also be suitable for a small embroidery if used alone; the embroidery is worked on linen with a muslin backing. Such an item is probably representative of the family involvement in each stage of its production as materials were hand spun and hand woven by members of the family. The bed hanging is thought to be late seventeenth century.

Eighteenth century silk embroidery on purses, gloves and pockets contains some exquisitely small design and stitchery, and the embellishment of clothes is worth looking at for its detail. This too was the great age of the sampler and it is in these earlier examples that we can find inspiration for our own attempts at small scale work. The nineteenth century was often more limited in its approach to stitchery, but tiny motifs are interesting, and some of the geometric patterns of Victorian samplers are useful.

Every age and civilisation produces some small artefacts which contain embroidery, and our museums yield many fine examples. Bead and embroidered purses and belts from the native peoples of North America show superb use of simple geometric designs. Collars and other accessories from Scandinavia have very fine pulled work on muslin. Both counted thread and blackwork

North American Indian purse of porcupine quills and beads.

techniques have always been highly adaptable for miniature designs, and the tiny birds, insects and fruits found on these are interesting in themselves.

For 250 years small textile pieces have been produced for dollshouses and these may be seen in collections in many parts of the world. Equal skill has been expended on clothes and accessories for dolls. It is interesting to note that with both these items the children who perhaps played with them have become the adult collectors who are both making and buying the finest crafted pieces to add to their own collections. The challenge of miniature stitchery and construction is probably at its greatest for collectors trying to furnish and dress dolls and dollshouses in appropriate fabrics.

Quite a few museums and organizations such as the Embroiderers' Guild are adding to their contemporary collections, and amongst their purchases have been some excellent examples of miniature embroidery, especially three dimensional and soft sculpture pieces. Much of the work that has been done, however, in this century has been personal, rather than for exhibition and sale, and remains in private hands. The purse illustrated is a good example of this, having been made in the 1920s and kept by the embroiderer's daughter. It is worked in silk on canvas, and is particularly effective because of its bare canvas background. The diagonal trellis is worked in tent stitch, moving in the direction of the diagonal, and this provides a pleasing foil to the added motifs of flowers, butterfly and ladybird.

Small purse. Tent stitch in silk on canvas. English, early twentieth century. 10 × 7.6 cm (4 × 3 in.). Owned by Hannah Taylor.

The purpose of this book is to deal with our own experiments in stitchery, but I hope that in trying out new techniques and increasing your experience of conventional ones you will look again at historical examples with new eyes. Also, although it is not very satisfying to copy slavishly, you can learn a great deal from the embroideries seen in museums and stately homes. It is very enjoyable to look at old embroidery books whenever you can find them. From the pattern books and herbals of seventeenth century England to the encyclopedias of stitchery that were popular in the 1930s there is inspiration to be gained for everyone.

2 Materials

As embroiderers you have a wide choice of fabrics, threads and other materials from which to choose. The contemporary interest in a multi-media approach also encourages a looking beyond traditional sources. Selecting materials will necessarily be related to the design and the techniques that are suitable for the project, as is true of any kind of embroidery. Working in miniature poses certain constraints because of the size, but it also gives us the chance to experiment with a wide variety of materials, since such small quantities are needed for any one item. The following guidelines will apply to much of our embroidery, and I have tried to isolate the most important considerations for miniature work.

(1) *The handling qualities*—Many miniature items are likely to be subject to considerable handling. Always consider the following:

- Will the fabric attract dirt easily, because of its composition or colour? Some synthetic fabrics become soiled very easily.
- Will the fabric deteriorate by being handled constantly?

Your ability to answer these must depend on experience, but it is always helpful to share this kind of information with others when a particular kind of fabric has not come up to expectations.

(2) *The cutting qualities*—With miniature embroidery accuracy is often essential, and some fabrics are difficult to cut into small pieces. Handwoven wools, or fabrics with a 'slub' effect in the weave may well pose problems like this, and wherever possible it is better to withdraw a thread to establish the true grain of the weave. Most evenly woven fabrics are easier to cut because their basic threads are visible, but some synthetic fabrics may distort with cutting. If straight edges and shape are important it is better to cut down the length of the selvedge as the warp threads (going parallel with the selvedge) stretch less than the weft threads (at right angles to the selvedge). Tearing fabrics produces a straight grain but this is difficult to do for a small piece. You need to ask:

- Will the fabric fray if you require it to do so, or fray if you don't want it to?
- Is it easy to cut straight lines or curves?

Samples of fabrics available with miniature patterns.

(3) The sewing qualities—When we are concerned with finer techniques and small scale stitchery the following questions become more relevant:

- How adaptable is the fabric to a variety of techniques or will its use restrict the type of embroidery? Obviously counted thread must be worked on an evenly woven fabric. Make

19

sure that there are the same number of threads per centimetre or inch on both warp and weft or a square design will finish up as a rectangle! Experiment with techniques on what appear to be unsuitable fabrics and see whether anything new and exciting can be worked. Canvas, despite its association with counted stitches, can be very versatile and, particularly when used for miniature, provides a good rigid background for a variety of techniques.

- What types of needles and pins are suitable? It is best to use the smallest needle which will take the thread, and with which you feel comfortable. Fine needles can be used instead of pins and are not as likely to mark. Also, never leave pins or needles in the fabric for any longer than necessary.
- Will the fabric crease easily? The combination of natural fibres with synthetic threads has given a great versatility to what is available and improved the wearing qualities considerably. But the effect of the artificial fibre often means that the fabric will not produce a neat, crisp crease. When working in miniature this becomes more obvious and a crucial factor for techniques like patchwork or for tiny constructed items.

(4) *Construction qualities*—When working in miniature many different questions arise owing to the small scale work involved, but the construction qualities of the fabric are still relevant:

- Is the fabric sufficiently opaque when placed over a backing card? Even careful stitchery can show through from the back in the wrong places if the fabric is thin. Sometimes it may not be suitable to add another fabric either before or after the embroidery, so an additional backing must be made out of interfacing fabrics or even thin card or paper. Cut this to the exact size of the embroidery to prevent its being too bulky.
- Is the fabric strong enough to be stretched tightly on a rigid backing? It is often more difficult to stretch tiny pieces because you cannot grasp so much material at one time. Using a backing fabric will help but look carefully at how bulky this will make the finished work.
- Will the fabric take glue, or should glue be avoided at all costs?

It is impossible to avoid all problems – indeed, embroidery would be rather dull if no challenges remained – but, if possible, experiment first on a small sample of the fabric.

Threads

All the same considerations apply to the threads you use. Such a rich diversity of yarns are available now, and many can be used for miniature embroidery. Even thick, heavily textured yarns

Sampler of Guilloche stitch on cotton lawn. Each row was worked with satin stitches 2 mm in depth. Threads used from top to bottom: sewing cotton, soft embroidery cotton, coton à broder, pearl cotton No. 5, crewel wool, divisible tapestry.

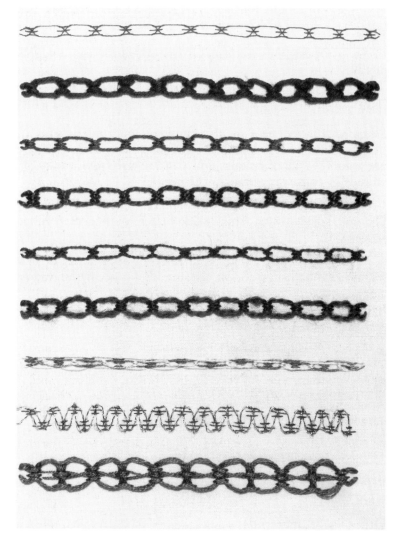

may be appropriate for some techniques and designs, although the finest of threads are usually best. There are so many varieties of yarn available, sold under different manufacturers' names, that it would be impossible to list them. The following list includes those that are most suitable for working in miniature:

Sewing threads These are made of cotton, synthetic fibres and metallics, and suitable for both hand and machine sewing. They produce fine, precise stitchery. Stronger threads are useful for making up items and with fine needles will make interesting knitting.

Crochet and lace threads These come in a variety of thicknesses and are of a good strength.

Soft embroidery thread This is used for couching, but tends to rub easily.

Coton à broder This has a good smooth finish and is highly flexible.

Pearl cottons These have a higher degree of twist, which gives them a distinctive finish.

Stranded cottons These are also known as embroidery 'silks' or 'floss' and are the most widely used of embroidery threads. There are a good range of colours and you can use from one to six strands of cotton at a time in the needle.

Cotton and linen yarns These have a flatter finish, but are usually fine and fairly strong. They work better for line than filling stitches.

Metal threads These range from fine synthetic yarns to best quality gold and silver. Some are suitable for needles and most can be couched.

Silk threads These have a distinctive beauty and work well in miniature.

Embroidery wools These range from fine crewel to thicker tapestry types. Some varieties have a slightly fluffy surface which becomes more obvious in miniature embroidery. The divisible wools have a tighter twist to them, good for flat canvas embroideries, particularly dollshouse carpets.

Knitting and weaving yarns Most of these are too heavy, but for couching and surface textures small amounts may be useful.

Ribbons All kinds of ribbon can be adapted easily for miniature work.

Other useful materials
There are many materials around us, often quite commonplace that can be incorporated into our embroidery if the design requires them. Some of these have particular advantages for miniature embroidery.

Paper When the embroidery is not going to be handled excessively, many kinds of paper can be used. Photographs are particularly suitable for small scale embroideries where an embroidered frame can be made. To secure the photograph take a fine matching sewing cotton and a sharp fine needle. Come up through the backing fabric and down into the corner of the photo with a stab stitch which will secure it quite firmly.

Metal and plastic meshes These can be cut without fraying and be used as base fabrics; they are adaptable for many kinds of stitchery. Look for them at your local greengrocers where they come in a variety of colours and meshes. The more rigid meshes are good for small, three dimensional embroideries.

Interfacing and bonding fabrics These may be either iron-on or sew-in varieties and are useful in miniature work where extra rigidity is required or fraying needs to be prevented. They will, however, also reduce the flexibility of the fabric, so experiments should be made before the embroidery is worked.

Water soluble fabrics These can either be immersed in cold or boiling water and will disappear leaving a lacy fabric. The embroidery for this is best done on the sewing machine and all the threads must inter-connect for the 'lace' to be held together.

Beads, sequins and sequin waste The discreet use of these on small embroideries can give interesting raised effects, particularly in creating 'flowers' for landscapes and gardens.

Found objects Small pieces of stone and wood have been successfully used in embroidery, but when working in miniature

*'Anyone for tennis?'
Tennis racquet and
shoes from key ring,
vegetable nets, stitchery
in soft embroidery
cotton. 10 × 7.5 cm
(7 × 4¼ in.).*

care should be taken not to overweight the design. In gift and toy shops there are many small, interesting accessories which can be used where suitable. Many of these tiny items are found on key rings, and include tennis racquets, clocks, skis and household objects. Model shops also stock a large range of accessories, such as fences, walling, ladders and seats, which could be used. Keen miniaturists will be accustomed to looking for articles that suit their particular scale in every likely and unlikely place.

Constructed fabrics There are occasions when even the finest turnings or seams are unsuitable and therefore you must construct fabrics for the purpose, either as a background to work on, or as an applied part of the design. Fine knitting can be worked with two or three-ply wool, or with a thick sewing cotton. Using 2 mm needles, any variations on pattern knitting can be achieved, although with such fine thread the result tends to be more 'lacy' than usual. Crochet or tatting or netting could also be useful. Simple weaving is effective for small areas and can be worked on a thick piece of card matching the thickness of threads to the required texture of the piece. Strong sewing cotton will be adeqate for a warp on a small piece with fine wool, or embroidery threads for the weft. Constructed pieces like these can easily be attached to a backing card or fabric.

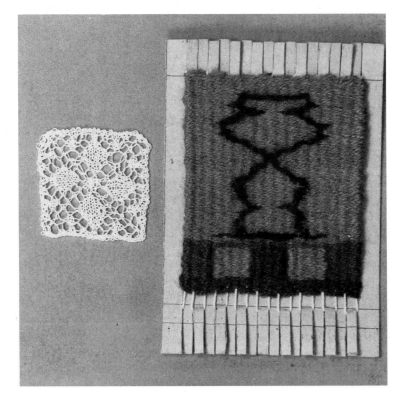

Constructed fabrics. Knitting on four 2 mm needles with No. 60 crochet cotton. 5 cm (2 in.) square. Ruth Caudwell. *Tapestry weaving on card using fine wool. 9.5 × 8 cm ($3\frac{3}{4} \times 3\frac{1}{4}$ in.)*

The store cupboard

I have never met an embroiderer who could resist the temptation of collecting threads, fabrics and useful accessories. Look again at what you have in the store with an eye to its use in miniature embroidery. The following list includes basic tools and accessories:

— small, sharp pointed embroidery scissors and large fabric scissors
— pencils, rulers, felt tips, etc. for drawing and design
— metal ruler and craft knife for cutting card
— card from cereal packs, small card boxes, photographic mounts
— any small frames of whatever material, i.e. plastic, metal, wood
— glues for paper and fabric, with white PVA glue being the most useful
— double-sided sticky tape and masking tape
— button or linen thread for lacing embroideries on to card
— spare pieces of fabric left from dressmaking or other household uses, such as interlinings, ribbons, tapes, felt, vegetable nets
— postcards and photographs which appeal to you, especially the tiny colour photographs found in colour brochures
— pages from the colour supplements to cut up for design ideas
— needles of different sizes; much depends on personal preference here but try to use the smallest you can to do the job efficiently. Standard sizes are available in many shops but for specific requirements it is always worth trying to find help from specialist retailers (often to be found in the appropriate magazine); alternatively, contact the needle manufacturers. Always look in old fashioned haberdashery shops for items that may·have gone off the market.

Types of needles

Betweens or *quilting* needles are short with round eyes and are used for quick, even stitching.

Embroidery or *crewel* needles are longer and have larger eyes to take one or more strands of thread.

Sharps have short round eyes, useful for general sewing.

Tapestry needles have blunt points and can take thick threads to very fine ones, depending on their size; they are used on canvas or even weave fabrics.

Chenille needles have large eyes and sharp points. They can take heavier threads and will pierce thick fabrics. They are most useful if a couching thread has to be taken through to the background of the fabric.

Beading needles are very long and fine and very flexible.

Circular needles are particularly useful in the construction of miniature items, and it is worth buying a set in assorted sizes. It is sometimes possible to acquire surgical circular needles which are much finer, and for this you may have to search amongst your friends for the right source!

Many of the *heavier darning* or *carpet* needles are not generally needed for miniature work.

3 Inspiration for design

The sources for embroidery designs are all around you and before
considering design in greater detail it is worth contemplating the
rich resources available. There are two ways in which you can
look for ideas that will work well in miniature. Firstly, you could
take a larger picture and reduce it to a small scale version, as is
often done with garden scenes or landscapes. Persian miniatures
and the rich details of medieval illuminated letters have this
quality of containing many small, fine details in a limited space.
Secondly, you could focus on what is miniature in the surround-
ing world and reproduce that in detail. Some examples that
immediately come to mind are butterfly wings, the grain in wood,
marks in stone, brick and surface patterns on buildings, and
petals of a flower.

In the later section on design I shall look more closely at the
many resources available, but this is a general list of good starting
points.

(1) Colour postcards and photographs are on sale in the many
gardens, stately homes and museums. Personal photography
is useful for capturing the scenes and ideas that appeal; they
do not need to be of professional standard to serve as an aid to
memory later on.

(2) The colour supplements with newspapers and quality magazines have excellent photographs. Also, you can use such
paper for creating abstract designs.

(3) Patterned fabrics with suitable designs may suggest ideas for
stitchery, be useful as background fabric or be used for
appliqué or patchwork.

(4) Particular threads may have interesting colours or textures
which will suggest the use of a design in relation to a certain
technique.

(5) Direct drawing from immediate surroundings and nature is
useful if notes are kept of colour, texture, etc. with quick
sketches. Good notes will more than compensate for lack of
drawing ability.

(6) Drawing round outlines of objects can be a good starting point, such as pegs, curtain rings, pastry cutters, leaves, flowers, vegetables or anything that appeals. Prints can also be taken from leaves.

(7) Rubbings can be made from tree bark, concrete, stones, rough wood or walling, using soft pencils (4–6B) or the wax crayons used for brass rubbing.

Design resources for specific projects

It is sometimes helpful to look for specific details when interested in a particular project, and the following list is concerned with those items that may well be the subject for miniature embroidery.

Jewellery Museums (for example, the Burrell Collection in Glasgow and the Victoria and Albert Museum in London) provide good examples, with contemporary magazines and exhibitions for looking at jewellery which may be materials other than precious metals. When looking for inspiration remember that jewellery must hang correctly and look suitable. Similar considerations also apply when you want to decorate the Christmas tree!

Brooches in leather and metal threads. Each approximately 4 cm ($1\frac{1}{2}$ in.). Pat Harper.

Three dimensional embroideries Catalogues, particularly Christmas editions, will provide a rich source for tree decorations, mobiles and advent calendars. Museums provide ideas for boxes, sculpture, gloves, etc. The executive toy as an embroidered piece can be given a little wit and humour, just as the child's toy can be designed to give pleasure and have tactile qualities.

Doll and dollshouse accessories Here the aim is to provide a small scale replica of the clothes and furnishings to be found in a real house of the period. Room settings in museums, contemporary paintings, drawings and photographs will give colour and details. Contemporary books may describe the way household items were made or used. Magazines devoted to the collecting of dolls and dollshouses are particularly helpful. The intention is to convey the 'feel' of the period. It is worth remembering that only

Dollshouse embroidery frame with silk embroidery on silk gauze at 48 threads to 2.5 cm (1 in.). Embroidery 2.5 cm (1 in.) square. Embroidery by Cynthia Jacobs. *Frame by* Cliff Herbert.

the richer section of the population usually had their houses painted or photographed and avant-garde ideas took longer to filter down into the ordinary home.

Sewing accessories and small gifts These will include cases for needles, scissors and spectacles, pin cushions, small purses, bookmarks, etc. Old embroidery books are good for basic techniques and stitches which can be developed in a modern way.

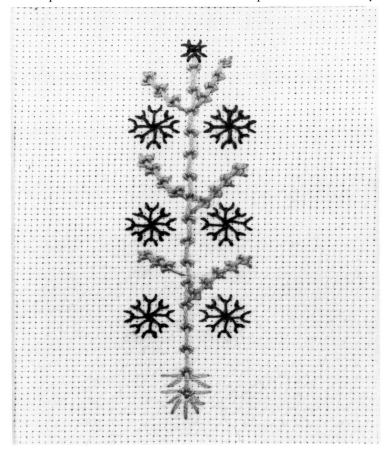

Flower spray. Evenweave fabric. Fly and Cretan stitches in stranded cotton and coton à broder. 13 cm (5 in.) long. May Plummer.

Greetings cards The joy of receiving a hand-embroidered card compensates for the work involved. Look for decorative letter forms which can be incorporated into the design, using these in an abstract or realistic way. Rich, colourful fabrics may be a source of inspiration in their own right, with bright impact as the key to the final design.

Small pictures Many sources will be relevant here, but it is worth looking at the personal aspect. A scrapbook of photographs or cuttings, with ideas from embroidery exhibitions, is a constant source for future reference, as are samples worked at dayschools or on courses.

4 Basic priorities for design in miniature

Designing for embroidery is often seen as intimidating, yet all around are examples, from which you make your choice in clothes, domestic furnishings and houses. On a larger scale you make judgments on the landscape you live in, the planning of gardens and towns. Just as you choose what appeals to you, what is right for the purpose, the same is true of embroidery. When working in miniature the same considerations apply, but these are sharpened by the limit in size. Two questions are relevant:

- What is the purpose of the article?
- What effect are we trying to achieve?

Greetings card.
22 thread canvas.
Darning, satin stitch,
French knots in pearl
cotton. 11 × 7 cm
(4½ × 3 in.).
May Plummer.

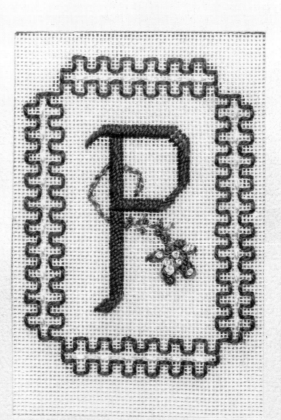

When considering the purpose you need to know whether the embroidery will be handled by a child or adult; be placed on a wall; be freestanding; be seen in the context of other items or be seen on its own. In thinking about the effect you are trying to achieve think about whether the embroidery should make a strong visual impact despite its small size. Will it encourage the viewer to look closely at its detail? Or is it trying to emphasize a particular technique, thread, fabric or colour.

Two examples will show how these are interrelated. A greetings card must be rigid enough to stand up on its own, be suitable for the occasion, and have a visual impact from at least a short distance away. A dollshouse bedspread, however, must blend with its surroundings, must lie flat, have the right surface texture and be correct in its proportions.

OPPOSITE
Dollshouse bedspreads in assorted patchwork techniques. Photography and embroidery by Carol Black.

Christmas card. 12 thread canvas. Ribbons, pearl cotton, sequins, wool. 14 × 10 cm (5½ × 4 in.).

OPPOSITE
Dollshouse bedspreads – scale of 1 in. to the foot. Photography and embroidery by Carol Black.

*Medieval lady. Design
based on brass rubbing.
Evenweave fabric. Half
cross and straight stitch
in coton à broder.
13 × 11 cm (5 × 4 in.).
May Plummer.*

The basic priorities in design are not a mystery, but simply the choices made when you start a new embroidery project. These are dealt with in more detail in subsequent chapters, but design criteria can be summarized as follows:
(1) simplicity of design;
(2) suitability of techniques, fabrics and threads;
(3) construction;
(4) finishing and framing.

These necessarily overlap one another, and when seized with a new idea you are not necessarily conscious of each stage. Other elements will help in achieving both impact and the desired effect:

Texture Quality of surface is as important in small as in large embroideries. It is tempting to handle embroidery which is texturally interesting, and hopefully much miniature embroidery will not always be behind a label reading 'do not touch'.

Colour The eye must focus on what is important without the overall impression of the piece being diminished. Any colour choice can be judged from a distance if you look through half-closed eyes. In certain types of miniature embroidery the choice of colour is critically important. Accessories for dolls and dollshouses need to reflect a particular period of history which has its own colour characteristics.

Scale Not only must the design look right in relation to the size of the finished embroidery, but the total measurements must be suitable for the purpose of the article. A needlecase must be large enough to take the needles, but it will be better used if it can fit into a handbag or workbox. The scale of the design and the maximum size of the embroidery need to be closely related.

Abstract or realistic The aim of each piece of embroidery must surely be the viewer's appreciation of its design, execution and final purpose, so it is not important whether the finished result is representational or abstract. In some circumstances a realistic picture is desirable or necessary, but often natural forms such as minerals, plants and landscapes can lend themselves to being treated in an abstract way. This, too, may give more freedom in the choice of colour and technique.

It is important that the basics of design are heeded but not slavishly followed. The inspiration of a drawing, photograph, fabric or thread is creative in itself and from there, with some thought, the embroidery can develop its own life. This piece by Barbara Laing is a good example of this. The original inspiration was a mossy section on paving slabs in a courtyard garden. It combines simplicity of design with appropriate stitchery, and the result is pleasing to the eye. It also combines the two aspects of

35

miniature embroidery that I find continually fascinating – immediate impact, when you view it as a whole, yet fine detail, which can be appreciated on closer inspection.

Pavement design.
Calico, with variety
of stitches and threads.
5.6 cm (2¼ in.) square.
Barbara Laing.

5 Experiments in design

Working to personally created designs should be an enjoyable part of embroidery and one that can be developed irrespective of skill. Producing miniatures means that large scale drawings are not required and that many design ideas can be sketched in a

Quick method of reducing the size of a design –
(1) Grid of squares drawn over original design;
(2) smaller squares and freehand drawing to required size.

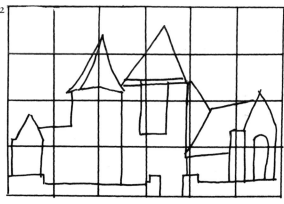

notebook and worked directly from there. To keep the focus on the miniature I suggest that you design to the approximate size of the finished embroidery. In this way you are constantly challenged by the need to simplify and to create the right impact.

The design ideas that follow in this chapter are not limited to use with miniature embroidery but all are helpful for focusing down to a small scale. These are mentioned as starting points and there will be many other ways in which suitable designs can be found. A clear, strong design is a guide for creative embroidery and should not be a fetter for it. The joy of working in miniature is that a sample can turn into a satisfactory finished item. I speak as one who hates doing samples for their own sake!

Obviously, there are occasions when the design on paper is the wrong size for the planned embroidery, and a reduction or enlargement must be made. This method is not too technical and will work adequately when precise measurements are not absolutely necessary. Make a tracing or photocopy of the design and divide this evenly into a grid of squares or rectangles. Draw the shape of the finished embroidery and divide this into the same number of divisions. Details can then be copied freehand from each section of the original design to the working drawing.

Designs using photographs

(1) If the photograph is of the required size, use greaseproof or tracing paper to trace over the main outlines. Household greaseproof is actually thinner, and more detail can be seen through it. If the photograph is rather pale in colouring, then 'Cling Film' wrapping paper can be used, and the details can be worked over with a thick felt tip pen. These thicker lines will then be visible through the greaseproof, and a second tracing can be made on which details can be added. Trace two or three of these basic line drawings so that experiments can be made. Otherwise, once the original tracing has been worked on it is no longer simple and clear. Placing two or three of these drawings side by side will help to suggest the most appropriate embroidery technique. Darker and lighter areas can be shaded in. It is better to have fewer lines and shaded areas at this stage and a good basic drawing. More detail can be added while the embroidery is in progress in reference to the original photograph.

(2) If the photograph is much larger than required and a section only is required for the embroidery, make a card mount with the cut out area of the size of the finished embroidery. Experiment by placing this over the photograph to isolate areas of the design which would be most suitable. Using a mount in this way can produce very pleasing abstract designs.

A card mount over a section of a photograph to isolate possible areas of design.

Foliage, rocks and building surfaces are good examples of this.

(3) Where the original source for the design is a slide transparency, this can be projected on to a wall where a piece of paper has been fixed. The main outlines can then be drawn on to the paper from the projected image. The projection from the slide can be made to the exact size required, but if this seems too small, then do a drawing and reduce it in size as suggested above.

Designs using cut paper
There are many ways of using cut, torn and folded paper as the source for embroidery design. When using these techniques it is best to focus on the miniature aspect of the finished embroidery.

Design based on overlapping circles.

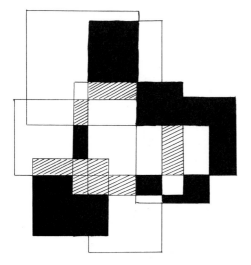

Design based on overlapping squares.

A rectangle of approximately 10 × 15 cm (4 × 6 in.) will make a good frame, or a circle to similar dimensions. As these can be adapted to all kinds of embroidery, concentrate on the simplicity and particular characteristics of working in miniature.

Coloured paper from photographs or magazines can be cut into realistic or abstract shapes. Cut a square or a circle out of paper, then divide this up and create a design from the pieces. This works particularly well for blocks of embroidery stitches, using techniques such as canvas work or pulled thread.

Textured designs can be created using folded paper, crumpled tissue or corrugated papers.

Counterchange is ideal for small simple designs for needlecases, dollshouse carpets or a greetings card. Take a symmetrical design, cut it in half, and reverse the tonal values in each half. A limited colour choice, even just two contrasting shades, works best for this kind of design.

Sixteenth century Swiss bedhead design adapted for a counterchange pattern.

Designs using paint and dyes

For a miniature embroidery, especially for greetings cards, paints and dyes are particularly relevant. Small areas of colour can be added where a flat surface is required, and this can then be highlighted with a minimum of stitchery. If the article is to be handled, such as a small purse or needlecase, then the correct fabric dyes must be used. Otherwise water colours, household dyes or water colour pencils can be used. More specific instruction can be found in general embroidery books and these can be adapted to work in miniature. Simple designs can be made by gluing string patterns on to a wooden block for printing. Small potato cuts or sticky shapes (as used by children for patterns) can be glued on to paper. Colour can be sprayed, painted on with a brush, stippled by flicking from a toothbrush or smudged on with a sponge. Small stencils cut from card are ideal for miniature designs. Always keep colours slightly more muted than required, as a strong colour may be offensive to the eye on a small embroidery; more impact can be added on the embroidery later. Techniques such as batik, tye and dye, or pleating may be more difficult to achieve in miniature but as a background fabric these can be useful at times. Beware of becoming too adventurous or as most of us discover at some time, the effect may just be too fussy for the scale of the project.

Sections of a pineapple –
(right) thin slice;
(left) enlarged drawing
of outer segments.

Drawing for design

It is unfortunate that many talented embroiderers feel inhibited by the idea of drawing out their own designs. Remind yourself

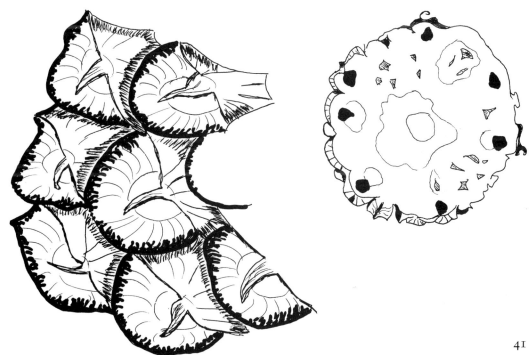

regularly that you are not trying to imitate fine art, but to make marks on paper which are useful and relevant for the embroidery which is the final product. This is where a notebook for reference is so useful to give rise to a constant stream of ideas. Finished miniatures may be either the whole of a design, such as a landscape reproduced to a small scale, or just a detail of it. Books on drawing and design will provide many ideas, but these are just starting points to encourage you to look more closely at what you see.

All around are shapes that can be drawn in simple line form, such as fruit, vegetables, trees, houses, buildings and architectural features. Do not be afraid of rough sketches, but equally do not be embarrassed about using a ruler. The important thing is to get basic shapes, patterns which are vital to the object being drawn, light and shadow, either as part of the drawing or as separate notes.

Many objects can actually be drawn round to give an outline, for example leaves, flowers or household items, such as pegs and scissors. The drawings can then be used for abstract or realistic designs. If a master copy is made on thicker card, this can be cut out and used as a stencil.

Two pastry cutters and a potato masher drawn in outline.

The adapted design.

*Drawing round outline
of simple leaf shapes.*

We all tend to doodle when we have an empty pad in front of us, usually when we are listening to a telephone conversation, or sitting through a committee meeting. Look at your own doodles, and develop the patterns that appeal to you, cutting them up, colouring them in and seeing what shapes can be created.

Exercise with a simple linear design

This basic design was adapted from a typical landscape design and was deliberately simplified to create some strong horizontal lines and one or two verticals. It can be used either way up, and the areas interpreted as freely as wished or omitted all together. It offers one possibility of looking at landscapes and buildings in different ways, and it is given as an example of how drawing can be simplified. It also shows how each of the embroiderers who

*Outline drawing for a
linear landscape.*

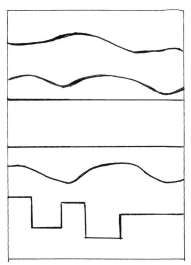

Four examples of the linear design for a landscape. Each one measures 10 × 8 cm (4 × 3 in.). Buildings – May Plummer

Pastoral landscape – May Plummer
Summer – Janet Russell
Design adapted for box top – Barbara Laing

took this design adapted it and made it quite unique to their own style.

There are four basic ways of starting with this design:
(1) With the vertical lines at the top a distant view of buildings can be created or perhaps cliffs or rock formations.
(2) With the vertical lines at the top a close up view gives quite a different perspective, and in the example given this was based on the roof and window patterns of a house.
(3) With the vertical lines at the base a wall or rock formation becomes apparent, with a distant view of a landscape.
(4) The close up view with the vertical lines at the base can be interpreted as a wall, paving, etc.

Uses for the linear landscape – variations using the vertical lines at the top.

The linear landscape – with vertical lines at the bottom.

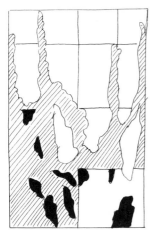

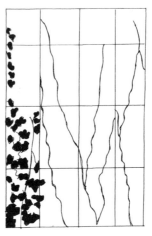

Two designs based on the window with ivy (See below left).

I was also looking for a way in which this design could be used in a completely abstract way and discovered that in fact it had seven sections. Out of this a rainbow effect was born which would make a good basis for a greetings card or the front of a needlecase.

Drawing exercises using windows, archways and doorways

Personal preference plays a large part in our choice of designs, and I particularly enjoy the challenge of recreating windows,

BELOW LEFT
Ivy seen through a window from the inside. Photography by Jean Brown.

BELOW RIGHT
Archway design. Calico, wadding, shaded silk in black and white, yellow. Italian quilting thread, grey chenille wool, dishcloth cotton. 11×9 cm ($4\frac{1}{2} \times 3\frac{1}{2}$ in.). Julia Simkin.

46

Drawing of window with decorative security bars.

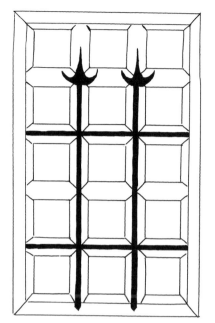

Archway drawing from a ruined abbey.

doorways and arches. These are very useful as design sources, as they provide a ready-made 'frame'. This allows a great deal of freedom for interpretation in both detail and technique. In our own immediate environment we can find many examples of these doors, arches, gateways and windows. These can be drawn out with a ruler to the required size, and then the detail can be added. The whole frame may be reduced to a miniature, or one section may be worked on. The examples given here illustrate a variety of these frames and show how they provide a useful focus when concentrating on the miniature.

Designs suggested by the fastenings on an art nouveau window.

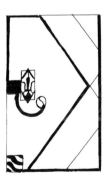

47

Design with fabric and thread

Most embroiderers are like magpies in their ability to acquire favourite pieces of fabric and thread. Look through these occasionally if you are seeking inspiration from colour or texture and work directly with them. Sort out small pieces which are suitable for miniature embroideries, or those with tiny patterns, and keep them in a separate bag for easy reference. In developing the following ideas, focus on the miniature, and other possibilities will start suggesting themselves.

One colour embroidery using different tones in fabric and thread can be effective in a small piece of embroidery, emphasizing the textural qualities of the materials used.

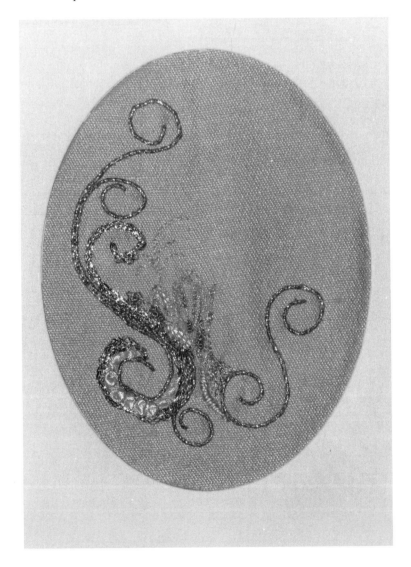

Greetings card. Blue slub fabric. Stitchery in couched gold, cotton and ribbon. 15.3 × 11.5 cm (6 × 4½ in.). Joan Botteley.

Embroidered dollshouse
made for a silver wedding
present. Worked on 18
thread canvas, stranded
cotton and beads. Stiffened to
make box-like construction
with hinged front and lined
inside. 17 cm wide x 18 cm
high x 12 cm deep (6¾ x 7½ x
4½ in.). *May Plummer.*

The Garden. Stitchery in variety of threads, applied and padded fabrics, beads and plastic 'stone wall'. 17.5 x 12.5 cm (7 x 5 in.). *Jean Brown*, loaned by Sue Barlow.

Ribbon landscape. Variety of ribbons, stitchery on bottom layer. Covered with white chiffon. Embroidery 14 x 10 cm (5½ x 4 in.).

The Yellow Field. Printed silk background, applied leather, machine stitchery. Size of embroidery 8 x 5.5 cm (3¼ x 2¼ in.). *Nancy McGuiness.*

Pincushion made from brown fabric, with padding, and stitchery in French and bullion knots, tufting, metal pins, wool, silk and cotton threads. Ceramic base—7.5 cm (3 in.) in diameter. *Sheila Fawkes.*

Knot garden. Fawn dupion
fabric box hinged lid,
decorated entirely in wool
and cotton French knots. Box
measures 15 cm (6 in.) in all
directions. *Elise Holmes.*

Painted strawberry, quilted on pink polycotton. Green painted leaves, outlined with running stitch decorated with beads. 10 x 8 cm (4 x 3 in.). *Alex Lilley at the age of 10*

Linear landscape design worked in variety of stitches and threads. 10 x 8 cm. (4 x 3 in.). *Jetta Reading.*

One stitch embroidery is once more in vogue and works particularly well in miniature. It is a useful method for a competition where small scale embroideries have been specified. There are now many excellent books which encourage the embroiderer to experiment with the stitches we tend to take for granted.

Doodling with thread can be very satisfying as the type of thread used will determine how it falls on the fabric. Couching is an ideal technique for this kind of spontaneous design. Areas created by the line of thread can be used for filling stitches or left to highlight the background fabric.

Patterned fabric may be a source of inspiration in itself, with personal memories such as weddings or christenings to suggest uses for particular materials. Make a paper mount with the centre cut to the size and shape of the finished project and place this over the fabric. You can then see whether one or more motifs of the patterns are suitable in size or proportion. Do not add too much embroidery but give some added interest to the design in colour or texture.

Colour and design in miniature

The colour values of any piece of embroidery are important, and in miniature the choice is even more crucial as there is limited space impact. General books on embroidery contain precise information on the relation within the colour spectrum. Here are a few guidelines which particularly apply to small scale embroideries.

Correct colour balance is important in miniature work as the eye of the observer will assess the whole embroidery at one glance even though further study shows more intricate detail. This does not mean that miniature embroideries have to be bland. Small spots of bright colour will appear as small bright spots so the intention must be deliberate. French knot poppies in a field are a good example of this. A minimum of sharp colour helps to enliven a design and this can usually be done by taking a detail in a colour from the opposite side of the colour wheel. For example, a small amount of colour from the red/purple range will enhance a design that is mainly in the green/yellow range. Even with the restrictions of a small embroidery, the 'temperature' of colour is important, so look at fabrics and threads to see whether they give a warm or cold impression. The design of a Christmas card is interesting in this respect. For a winter scene 'cold' blues and whites could be the choice, but the colours for Christmas are traditionally red and green, with rich possibilities for the use of fabric and thread.

One of the basic rules of colour choice is that cold colours will recede and hot colours come forward, and likewise pale and bright. If great depth is needed, therefore, in a miniature piece it is vital to look at the threads and fabrics to see whether there are sufficient variations to give the perspective needed. Lay out the materials chosen on a piece of card and look at them with half-closed eyes to see whether the right impact is being gained. A small landscape picture can have a great deal of depth without being fussy if the colours are chosen carefully and the eye is led back through the landscape into the far distance.

For reference purposes it is useful to have a colour wheel, and this can be made quite simply. Take the widest variety of hues possible from the paper of magazines and colour supplements and glue these down on card in the correct relation to each other to make a colour wheel. This can also prove an interesting exercise in canvas work as the range of suitable threads from which a selection can be made is wide.

Specific types of design

The subject matter for miniature embroidery is unlimited and inspiration for design will be found in many ways. Occasionally however, a specific type of design is needed for a particular project or subject. The ideas given in this section may help to focus your ideas on these.

Landscapes These are always popular and can range from realistic interpretations of a scene to abstract versions which in miniature emphasize the basic shapes and colours. Try to get the shape and feel of the landscapes. In Chinese art it is said that even though the rocks below the water do not show, it should be apparent that they are there.

Gardens Look at the detail for a change with the great variety of textures and colours that can be found. The shadowed areas beneath and between trees and plants are interesting in themselves.

Architecture This is an extremely good source of design for miniature embroidery and can be worked readily with fine threads and counted techniques such as blackwork. Concentrate on the basic shapes and the overall characteristic of the building.

Pets and animals Cats and dogs have long been popular as subjects for embroidery, and photography now makes the copying of a particular pet much easier. If it is to be a realistic portrait look carefully at the fur or hair, and make sure that the background is not too fussy or obtrusive.

ABOVE LEFT
Blackwork house.
Evenweave fabric.
Straight stitch, bullion
and French knots
in coton à broder.
10 × 9.5 cm (5 × 4 in.).
May Plummer.

ABOVE RIGHT
Cat. Evenweave linen.
Cross and straight
stitch in coton à broder
and stranded cotton.
8.5 × 6 cm (3¼ × 2¼ in.).
May Plummer.

LEFT
Head. Linen.
Straight, stem stitches
and French knots
in stranded cotton.
5 cm (2¼ in.) square.
May Plummer.

Human figures This is probably the area that most of us find difficult to draw. In a miniature embroidery figures may be merely indications with a few simple lines. For detailed miniature portraits, books on sketching will give advice on the right proportions of the human figure.

Abstract and geometric designs The pleasure of these is that they give freedom of colour and texture. Inspiration for geometric designs can be found in so many sources from around the world. The needlecase illustrated here has an interpretation of an Anatolian carpet design on one side. The other side is based on squares and uses variations of texture within a limited colour range to give it interest.

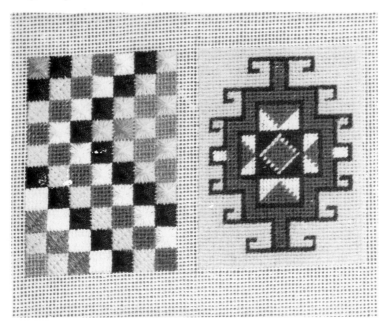

Two sides of a needlecase. Right – Anatolian design taken from a carpet. Tent stitch in wool and pearl cotton. Left – squares worked in Rhodes, Gobelin, reversed tent, tied diagonal stitches, using same threads. Each side measures 11×8.5 cm ($4\frac{3}{4} \times 3\frac{3}{4}$ in.). May Plummer.

Creating an atmosphere

In a miniature embroidery a major aim is to create something that will give pleasure to ourselves or to the recipient. This can include some witty statements about embroidery, and it is a joy at exhibitions to find pieces that can bring a smile. Atmosphere can be added in the way that Persian miniatures brought a rich quality to the stories they portrayed. The following ideas are offered in the hope that they may be the start of further ideas to give your projects a slightly different slant.

Symbolism was extremely important in Elizabethan embroidery, and messages could be conveyed by the use of personally identifiable designs. Patriotic feelings could be expressed in choice of fugres or royalty with symbols such as the pomegranate and the crown. The Elizabethans also loved playing with words, so family and personal mottoes were popular for small embroidered items. Our modern equivalent would be town or city badges, family crests, trade symbols or even family 'sayings'.

The atmosphere of a miniature embroidery needs to be carefully thought out at the design stage, and this can provide an interesting challenge. Technical 'tricks' used by the visual arts generally can help here.

- Dark skies with a light surround to the horizon or building will create a sense of foreboding.
- Tunnels, archways and porches create a sense of being closed in and looking through to something as yet unobserved. Look at some of the famous gardens to get ideas.
- A hint of looking round a corner, of flowers not always open, of buildings and features only half-glimpsed, gives a sense of depth and leads the eye further into the picture.
- An open landscape, garden or house is given a completely different atmosphere if foliage is added to the near foreground, such as waving grass or the hanging bough of a tree. This was once described to me by a photographer as a 'dingleberry' and it works as well in embroidery as it does in photography.

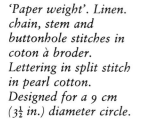

'Paper weight'. Linen. chain, stem and buttonhole stitches in coton à broder. Lettering in split stitch in pearl cotton. Designed for a 9 cm (3½ in.) diameter circle.

Witty statements are fun to work and in miniature can focus on something quite specific that appeals to us. This can include playing with words, such as the design illustrated for the paperweight. Observe the world around you, see how people work, children play and pets relax in their favourite places. Embroidery itself can create amusing ideas when names and meanings are considered. Look at a dictionary of embroidery stitches and consider the possibilities for 'gold bullion', metal thread 'chain', varieties of 'herringbone' and weather conditions expressed in 'wave stitch' or 'cloud filling stitch'.

Lettering for design in miniature

The use of lettering for small embroideries is highly satisfying and can be a simple and readily available source of design. The following questions need to be taken into account.

- Does the lettering need to be read as a whole word or sentence?
- Even if the lettering is used in an abstract form does it still need to be read as letters or can it just be the basis for the design?

There are no right or wrong answers to these questions because the solution will depend on your choice and on the function of the

Lettering designed for a photograph album. Size of each page in album 14.5 × 10.5 cm (5¾ × 4¼ in.). May Plummer.

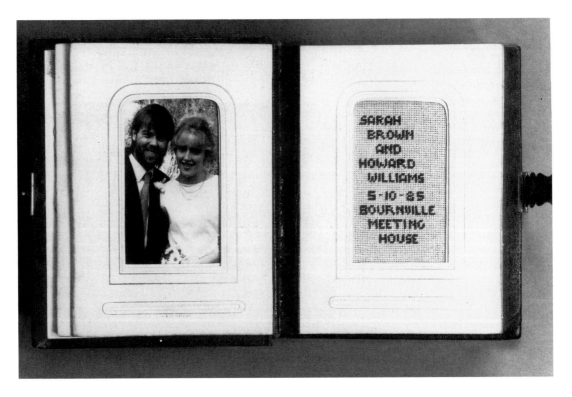

Sampler based on simple letter shapes. 18 thread canvas. Assorted stitches and threads. 8 cm (3 in.) square.

Sampler of letters and numbers. 22 thread canvas. Coton à broder. 10 cm (4 in.) square.
May Plummer.

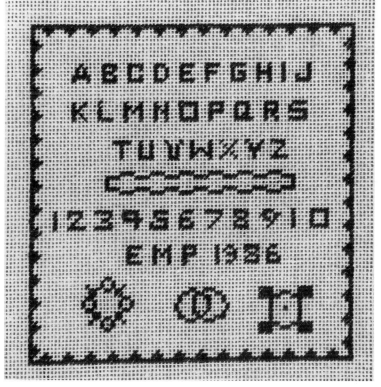

piece of embroidery. A name or a verse can make an extremely personal statement, but it is equally valid to distort lettering to create a pattern. The Chinese have used their calligraphy to illustrate poems in the form of bamboo leaves, and much of Islamic decoration depends on the versatility of the Arabic script. Books on calligraphy will give an idea of the large range to be found even within the Roman alphabet and will show how printers over the centuries have devised beautiful and ingenious ways of using our familiar letters and numbers. Specialist books on embroidery will provide ideas on how lettering can be adapted into stitchery. The richness of medieval manuscripts will suggest the multiple possibilities of working with a single letter in embroidery.

In some miniature embroideries, such as greetings cards, lettering must be a legible part of the design but not necessarily a dominant feature. A neat alphabet is useful for this, and two examples are included here. One is charted out for counted thread techniques and the other could be adapted for other kinds of stitchery. Both will work well on a very fine fabric or on a very small scale.

The following exercises will provide a starting point for using lettering or numerals as designs in themselves. Here, again, it is advantageous to work within a size that is more or less the same as the finished embroidery.

Chinese character for 'long life' by David Bass.

(1) Take a name, and write it in ordinary handwriting, then exaggerate the form of the writing, letting it flow freely. Shade in the areas between the letters or cut up the writing and rearrange the writing into a pattern.

(2) Take a rectangle, square or circle no more than 10 cm (4 in.) in any direction and divide it into smaller squares or segments. Write out one name, with one letter in each square, repeating it throughout the shape. Look at the patterns created by the letters. This can also be done by changing the directions of the letters in each square, or repeating just one letter or numeral throughout the shape.

(3) Take two letters and draw them at random in the shape of the design, with experiments overlapping the forms or keeping them separate.

(4) Cut out a letter from thin card, pin it to the centre of the design shape and rotate it round the pin, drawing the outline in various positions.

(5) Work on the idea of the illuminated letter from medieval manuscripts, embellishing it with extra lines, adding small motifs or pictures so it becomes a design in itself. The motifs

Design based on the name Anna by David Bass.

Chart for two alphabets by May Plummer.
TOP: *suitable for linear stitches such as running, chain, stem*
BOTTOM: *suitable for canvas, counted thread, cross stitch.*

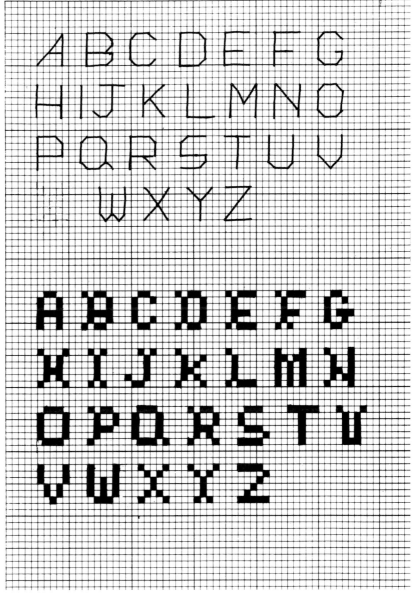

could be chosen to suit the letter, such as primroses or poppies to go with the letter P.

(6) Experiment with print cut from newspapers and magazines, or computer graphics, to see what designs are suggested by their particular forms.

6 Preparation for the embroidery

Too often it is necessary to produce a small present at the shortest possible notice. Then is the time to see what resources are available, to look through notebooks and scrapbooks for ideas and to assess what is practicable.

The finished embroidery may be in miniature but an adequate sized piece of fabric is needed for working on – one that can be attached to a small frame or worked in the hand in such a way that the embroidery does not become soiled or creased.

Think how the embroidery is going to be used, mounted or framed before cutting out the fabric, so that sufficient can be left round the working area. If a really small piece is to be used this can be sewn on to a larger piece of calico or sheeting, which will then go into the embroidery frame. A small rectangular picture frame can be used if a round ring frame is not available. Strong fabrics can be pinned to the frame. More delicate fabrics (or a more delicate frame) can be sewn round the edge of the frame for working. Small pieces of canvas do not need a frame, but to avoid distortion always take the needle right through the holes and then come up again in a separate motion, not bending the canvas to take the needle through in one action as in ordinary sewing. Tiny sections of canvas can also be attached to a larger piece of fabric and put into a frame; the fabric is then cut away beneath the centre of the canvas where the embroidery is to be worked.

Always make sure the fabric is clean and uncreased before the work is commenced. On a small embroidery any blemishes in the fabric will be more apparent. Look carefully at the weave of the fabric to make sure there are no uneven threads which will mar the design or prevent stitches from being worked evenly.

Make sure you buy enough threads to complete the whole design. If threads are being used from your own collection, always work small areas in one shade so that at least that section is complete. If the design is a landscape or similar, small changes in colour will not be so noticeable. If the design is more formal and geometric then changes will show up. If there is doubt about the amount of thread you have, always work small areas in each matching part of the design so that it will be symmetrical. Then if you have to change tone or colour, it will appear to be part of the original intention!

Transferring the design on to the fabric

Some of the traditional methods of transferring designs may be too cumbersome when you are working in miniature, but there are various ways of achieving a clear working design. These can be adapted to suit particular techniques and fabrics.

(1) On canvas or on pale fabrics where the embroidery will cover the design pencil or carbon can be used. Canvas can be placed over the design and a tracing made through; carbon can be used with caution if the fabric is not too delicate. A transfer pencil is suitable (where the design is drawn on to paper with the special pencil) if the fabric can take the heat necessary to iron on the design.

(2) A traced design can be cut up in section and each main area drawn or tacked round as a guide for the embroidery.

(3) Photocopies will print off on to pale fabric when pressed with an iron. Be cautious with this method as the iron must be hot enough to produce the imprint.

(4) A traditional method is to tack through a tracing of the design which has been drawn on greaseproof paper, which is thinner than tracing paper. The paper is pulled away leaving a tacked outline. To make the process easier pull a needle along the tacked lines on the paper – this will make the paper come away. On a miniature embroidery it is important not to have small pieces of paper left on the design. Keep the number of lines on the design to a minimum and use these as a starting point with the original design as a reference. If the tacking stitch is done neatly this could be left as part of the design.

(5) One method is particularly good for miniature embroidery whereby the design is drawn on the back of the fabric. If a dark fabric is being used it can be backed with a pale fine cotton. Using a stem stitch and working from the back, embroider the lines in the appropriate colours. This will produce a neat back stitch on the front. It can also be reversed with a stem stitch on the front. These lines can be left as part of the embroidery, embellished with other stitches, or used as the outlines for areas to be filled. Stitches need to be kept small and neat; be aware of the corners and curves to get the right effect. On a simple miniature such basic lines may be the major part of the finished embroidery and any variety of threads may be used to work with.

7 Techniques

Introduction

One of the joys of embroidery is that most techniques can be adapted to any level of skill. In this section of the book some ideas are suggested for working a variety of techniques on a smaller scale than usual. I am indebted to the many skilled embroiderers who have made miniature embroidery into a fine art and whose work and ideas have helped enormously in the preparing of this book. It would be impossible to discuss all techniques in detail, but I have tried to analyse the different kinds of embroidery and to suggest starting points and some practical hints.

Designs suitable for bookmarks, borders, etc. From top to bottom: Pompeii; fifth century Celtic; Medieval stone carving on tomb; and eighteenth century tapestry.

60

Abstract design adapted from a drawing of a rusting 'gas holder'.

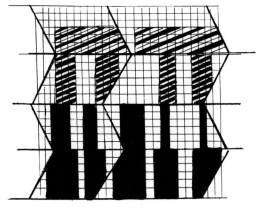

Within the scope of this book it would be impossible to describe all the basic instructions for each technique. In the bibliography there are books which give details of how stitches and techniques work. These and other books dealing with basic embroidery will help to increase your vocabulary of embroidery and give new inspiration.

Working samples

Small samples of different techniques can be useful, although I usually find that it is my successful embroideries that become the 'good' samplers and my failures that remind me of what did not work! Keep any experiments you make for future reference and note how long a particular technique took to work. Time is often a crucial element when you are faced with doing a piece of embroidery for a particular purpose, and some techniques can be very slow, such as pulled work on fine fabric.

Drawings from thin slices of agate.

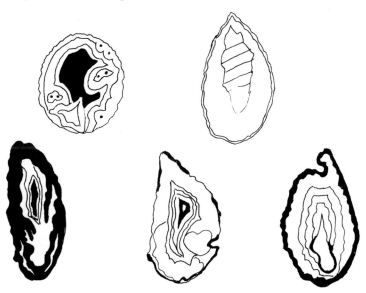

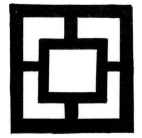
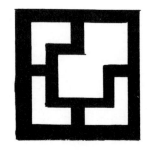
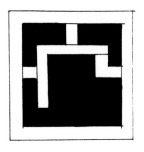

These variations on a theme are given to suggest ways in which our knowledge of different techniques can be extended. The two designs shown are based on simple drawings to show curves and straight lines in realistic, abstract or geometric sources. Work on a piece of fabric with the design area no larger than 10 cm (4 in.) in any direction to see what results can be achieved. The range of experiments will depend not only on skill and eyesight but on the sheer practical possibilities of putting thread, fabric and stitches together in miniature.

Take different background fabrics, looking at texture and the heaviness of the fabric. Experiment with a variety of threads on these from sewing cottons to knitting wools and see how the relation of the fabric and thread works in the design.

Concentrate on the linear aspects of the design, taking fabrics, threads and techniques that are suitable and see how well they work. Experiment with quilting, linear stitches like chain and buttonhole, couching, variations of running stitch, or the range of stitches on the sewing machine.

Use the areas created by the design, concentrating on filling these with a variety of techniques in different samples. These could vary from patchwork, to smocking, to pulled work and drawn thread, or depending on surface stitchery, using one stitch in many variations.

Concrete wall blocks – some broken.

Canvas work

It is inevitable that everyone has their own preferences in embroidery and I discovered a long time ago that I enjoyed canvas work (often known as tapestry in Britain or as needlepoint in North America). In recent years this kind of embroidery has been approached with a more adventurous spirit, and almost any kind of stitches can be used on canvas. Its advantage for working in miniature is that it is fairly rigid and can be used for three dimensional pieces. Also it can provide both frame and picture for a greetings card or small hanging, and there is a wide variety of canvas meshes and types to suit personal choice and the type of design. For those who prefer not to use a frame, canvas can also be embroidered easily in the hand and does not suffer unduly from being carried around in a bag. It can be cut easily and does

Dollshouse cushions.
22 thread canvas. Wool.
Each cushion is
approximately
2.5 cm (1 in.) square.
Margaret Prior.

not tend to fray, so it has uses for small mobiles, jewellery and Christmas decorations.

The gauge and type of canvas used will depend on the final purpose of the embroidery and one's own preference for fine detail. The course meshes are approximately ten threads to 2.5 cm (1 in.) and could be embroidered with ribbons and thick threads for a small embroidery based on a very simple design. Those most suitable for use with four- and two-ply wools, cotton or silk threads vary from 14 to 18 threads to 2.5 cm (1 in.). For fine detail a canvas of 22 threads to the inch is ideal, and although this makes excellent carpets for a dollshouse, many people find this too fine. For those with good eyesight gauzes can be bought from specialist shops which extend up to 54 or more threads to 2.5 cm (1 in.); for these gauzes fine silks need to be used or sewing cottons with a short tapestry needle of size 24 or finer.

It is quite acceptable to leave areas of canvas plain, to apply fabrics to certain parts of the design, or to paint canvas using

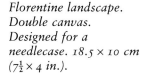

Florentine landscape.
Double canvas.
Designed for a
needlecase. 18.5 × 10 cm
(7½ × 4 in.).

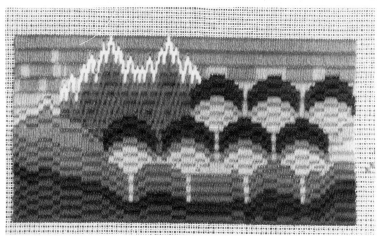

water colour or fabric dyes. At the other end of the spectrum to the fine gauzes are the plastic meshes – these can be used for quick effects and for items that need even more rigidity, such as Christmas decorations. Canvas work tends to be slow if only the traditional stitches are used such as half cross, tent stitch, etc. Experiment with Florentine (or Bargello) and straight stitches that cover the ground more quickly; try buttonhole, chain stitch and couching to get a variety of textures. Overlay decorative stitches on top of a flat, worked background.

When working on canvas get the size needle (always a blunt tapestry needle) that will take the thread but not distort the canvas; if you are using a two-ply wool on 18 canvas a size 24 tapestry needle is ideal. Never bend the canvas to get the needle through in one action as one does in ordinary sewing. This means that when working stitches such as chain, buttonhole or any other surface stitches they have to be completed in more than one movement but with a little practice this is an easy habit to acquire.

Designing for canvas work need not be difficult. Some embroiderers prefer to make a chart and work out each part of the design in detail. Draw out the design on graph paper, taking one square on the graph paper to each thread of the canvas, so the size of the design can be worked out and the design drawn or traced on. Then go over the design relating it to the threads of the canvas so that each part of the design is represented by one stitch or more on the graph paper. Do not be too concerned that curves appear to become straight lines, but allow the curve to move in small steps on the graph design. A curve can actually be seen once the embroidery is finished.

A free approach can also be taken, the design being drawn roughly on the canvas with a waterproof pen, or placed underneath the canvas for guidance as you work. Letter shapes, simple squares and rectangles work well on canvas and are ideal for items such as needlecases, belts, key tags, cards, etc. Persian carpets and Islamic designs adapt well and can be interpreted in a wide range of colours and threads. Perforated paper is available which is useful for bookmarks, but treat it with care while working and always cut a larger piece than required. Once the embroidery is finished cut back the paper, leaving an edge for the protection of the embroidery.

Some stitches, particularly those worked on the diagonal, will distort the canvas to some degree unless the canvas is worked on a frame. If there is distortion careful blocking will straighten the piece again. Always do this gradually and never be too impatient. Put the canvas, when finished, face down on a thick clean towel on a rigid surface and with a wet cloth (wrung out) gently press it on the back with a moderately hot iron. Pull the canvas at the sides, not at the corners, to get it back into shape, then press it

Drawing of hydrangea head adapted for canvas work, showing how the shapes can be 'squared' to fit the canvas threads.

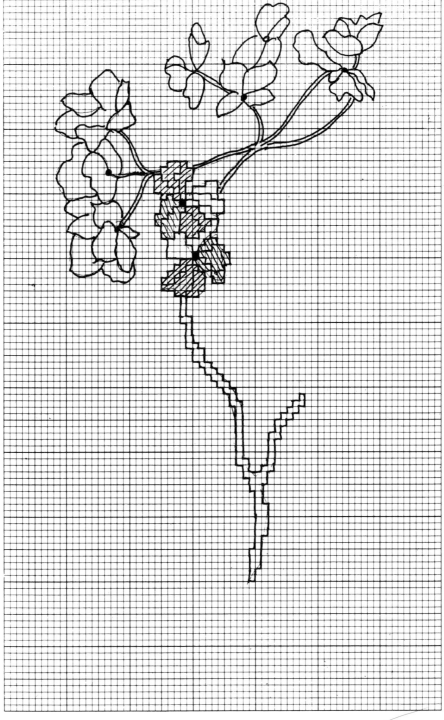

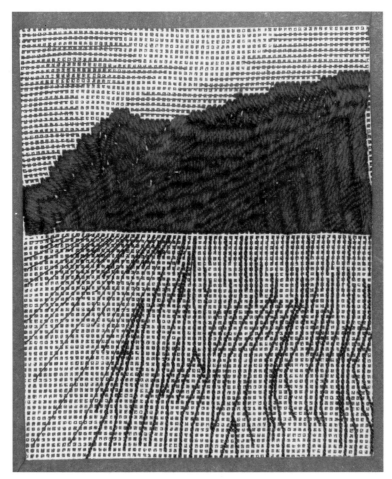

Black beach. Rug canvas. Darning and straight stitches in soft cotton, sewing thread and pearl cotton.
15 × 12.5 cm (6 × 5 in.).

again. Measure the diagonals with an accurate ruler: both the diagonals should measure the same. Don't repeat the blocking process too many times in one session. If the canvas will come only moderately into shape, pin it into the towel and leave it to cool and dry. Then repeat the process a few hours or even a day later.

Canvas work can be very bulky at the edge if it is to be turned over card or hardboard. Whatever the stitches used for the main design it is preferable to finish the edges with a half cross stitch as this gives a flat, neat, firm finish to the piece.

Dollshouse carpets embroidered on canvas have proved a good way of reproducing the full scale in miniature. I have included one example to show how an original design can be simplified and how important it is to get the colour balance right. The carpet, which is illustrated in colour plate 1a, is a one-twelfth version of a Baluch prayer rug measuring 150 cm by 90 cm (approximately 5 ft by 3 ft). The carpet was made in the mid-twentieth century but reflects the traditional sombre colours and designs of Baluchi

Chart for working the Baluchi prayer rug. The symbols denote the colours in the original:
Red: ☐ (14)
White: ⊡ (7)
Black: ■ (7)
Orange: ⊠ (2)
The amounts given in brackets are the approximate lengths required in metres or yards for working the design in half-cross stitch on 18 thread canvas. For this type of canvas one strand of a divisible wool or all six strands of stranded cotton are suitable.

carpets. In this one the central section seemed the most important in conveying the design of the original in a miniature version. It was worked on canvas with 18 threads to the inch, using a stranded two-ply wool. This design could also be used for the front of a needlecase or a greetings card, and be worked in silks or metal threads. If it were worked on a larger mesh canvas it could be adapted for a case or purse. For an even finer rug or to be hung on a wall of a dollshouse the canvas could be one with more threads to the inch, perhaps even a gauze worked with sewing cotton or fine silks. Stranded cotton works well for dollshouse carpets and gives a slight sheen to the finish. On this example one strand of a divisible two-ply wool was used. If stranded cotton is used, all six strands would be needed working half cross stitch to give an even finish to the embroidery. Quantities needed for this sized carpet are small and no more than one 8 metre (9 yard) skein is needed in any of the colours.

The following general instructions apply not only to dollshouse carpets but also to miniature canvas embroideries of this type.

(1) When working from a chart, it is advantageous to mark out in pencil the plain canvas with a centre line horizontally and vertically.

(2) The design can be started anywhere, but it is easier to work from the centre out to the borders.

(3) Half cross stitch is perfectly adequate for dollshouse carpets and small embroideries which will not be subject to hard wear. Some people prefer to work tent stitch or its continental version, which is worked diagonally. The latter is ideal for covering large plain areas.

(4) When beginning, knot the thread; leave this knot on the front of the work about 2 cm (1 in.) away from the start of the embroidery so that the stitches will cover the thread as they are worked. Then the knot can be cut off neatly. Always weave ends in as the thread is finished to prevent them being brought to the front accidentally or getting in a tangle on the back.

(5) Colours can be taken across from one part of the design to another but never more than 2 cm ($\frac{3}{4}$ in.) across. If the back is to be left uncovered then the stitchery must be as neat as possible.

(6) Finishing off the dollshouse carpet is very much a matter of personal preference. Some embroiderers leave the back uncovered and work in the edge by folding back the canvas on itself before the outer rows are completed. By working through two layers of canvas a neat edge is obtained, and then the outer border can be finished with oversewing. I prefer to work the design to the edge on the single thickness of canvas, then press the carpet and fold the canvas over, leaving two threads for the edge. I then work this with oversewing, long-legged cross stitch or buttonhole. If buttonhole is used on the short ends it makes a convenient loop for knotting in a fringe. The back may be covered with iron-on interfacing either before the edge is worked or ironed on inside the edge when this has been completed.

Other counted thread techniques

These will include amongst others, cross stitch, blackwork, Assisi, and pulled thread embroidery. All these can be attempted in miniature, but for regular, traditional counted work it is necessary to look for even weave fabrics whose threads match the weight of the embroidery threads used. A free approach is possible, so experiment with scrim, finer hessians, muslin and nets of all kinds. Stranded cottons, coton à broder and pearl cotton in the finer weights, crochet cottons, lace threads and sewing cottons can all be used and will give a variety of textures. There are some interesting metallic threads available, often used for the sewing machine but ideal for highlighting counted thread work. Some of these do not always lie flat on the fabric so try them out with different kinds of stitches. These techniques also combine well with other stitchery.

Cross stitch designs can be charted out like canvas work or used more freely. If you want to work cross stitch on a fabric where the weave is not clearly visible it is possible to create a mesh to work over. Many books suggest that pieces of canvas can be used and then withdrawn afterwards leaving neat stitches. I have found this method laborious and have experimented by creating a mesh from threads. The background fabric needs to be held rigid in a frame. Across this make a net (both vertical and horizontal) of threads, preferably of a smooth variety such as coton à broder or a polyester sewing thread. The net can be made to the size

BELOW LEFT
Blackwork skyscraper. Evenweave. Blackwork stitches in fine pearl cotton. 10 × 9.5 cm (4 × 3¾ in.).

BELOW RIGHT
Cutlery. Evenweave. Assisi worked in stranded cotton and coton à broder. 15 × 10 cm (6 × 4 in.).

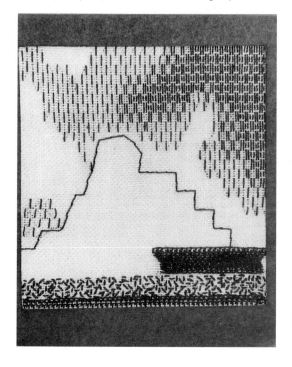

required and the spaces created for the cross stitch can also be varied. Work the cross stitch and then withdraw the threads. These can also be designed to be left in as part of the design. For a similar effect where the net can be left in position use pieces of old net, or the vegetable meshes that can be obtained from the greengrocers. These also have the advantage that they can be cut away without fraying to be part of the design where needed.

Blackwork is extremely effective in miniatures and gives a good clear picture for many subjects. Areas of shading can be built up, using a simple pattern such as a cross to begin with, then more stitches added. Remember that in miniature, if the design becomes too 'black' the effect of the pattern will be lost. Sewing cotton is ideal for working on fine fabrics and creating tiny patterns and pictures as it does not fluff and will lie flat on the fabric. Different weight threads can be used to add interest without making the design too complicated.

There are many stitches within the 'family' known as pulled work or drawn fabric, where the threads are not withdrawn but are pulled aside to make the lacy patterns. Worked in miniature these need a strong coloured backing to get the effect of the embroidery. It is also better to use only one or two variations of this within one small design as the background fabric will not be seen if the areas of stitchery are very small and complex. For transparent effects it could be mounted without a backing fabric in a clear plastic photograph frame or hung within a metal frame against a window. Pulled thread is very good for details of architecture, especially the geometric shapes to be found in Islamic art. For inspiration, look at the fine Swedish pulled work of the seventeenth and eighteenth centuries with tiny patterns in simple areas of design. Couching can also be added in a suitable weight thread to delineate certain motifs.

Stitches and their variations
There is so much variety in the use of simple embroidery stitches that we cannot finish exploring the possibilities. Some of the basic ways of using stitches are given in this section.

Using only one stitch
The simplicity of this approach is useful for tiny designs, and a variety of threads add interest to the stitch chosen. A limited colour range may also be chosen, with the design interest arising from the change in size, direction and texture of the stitch. Or the stitch may be kept to one size only but embroidered in a rich scheme of coloured threads. This is well-illustrated in the colour photograph of Elise Holmes' knot garden box (colour plate 7).

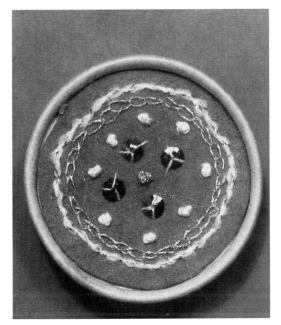

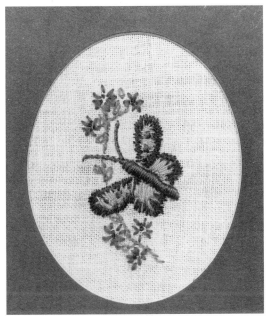

ABOVE LEFT
*Little box lid
embroidered by*
Margaret Priestman
*(aged 90). Box lid
diameter 5.5 cm (2 in.)*

ABOVE RIGHT
*Crewel embroidery.
Linen. Wool in straight,
stem, satin and chain
stitches. Size of motif
3.5 × 6 cm (1½ × 2¼ in.).*
May Plummer.

Crewel work

There has been a revival of interest in crewel work in recent years, and many people are attracted by the Jacobean designs. It is a pity, however, if these are interpreted only in faded, washed-out colours. In miniature, much of the detail of the filling stitches may be lost, so it is better to concentrate on one motif if it is going to be used for a card or the top of a box. One strand of crewel wool or silk can be used, and shading can be successfully achieved if you look for a range of threads which come in closely related colours. Use areas of couching, outlined with chain or stem stitch, with simple fine lines for leaf scrolls and stems. Try out more modern designs such as a picture of your own house or a favourite flower.

Couching

Even in miniature embroidery there is a place for thicker threads to provide interesting textures. Couching provides an ideal way of using threads such as metallic finishes, chenille, thick silks or weaving yarns. The couched line can be kept flat, or bunched to make a raised texture. It can also be used for filling areas of the design. A map is an interesting source for a design, with contour lines kept as single couching, and areas such as hills, rivers or city plans being treated as filled areas.

One particular kind of couching that has always been associated with fine embroidery is that of ornué: here the strands of silk or metal thread are laid across the area to be covered, then the design is worked in the colour of the tying-down threads. It is a

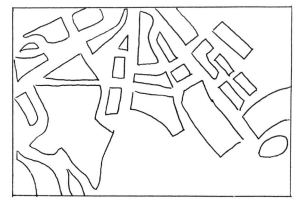

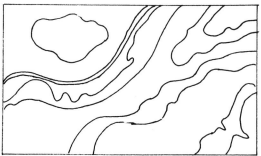

Two maps adapted as designs for couched embroidery.

time-consuming method, but with metallic threads underneath the silk, the richness of colour and texture is extremely effective. It works very well for miniature embroidery, as small details can be worked into a tiny motif. The background fabric is traditionally covered entirely by the couching, but in a modern adaptation some of the background fabric could be left showing. The design can be drawn or tacked on to the background fabric, and each row of couching must be completed with its tying down threads before the next row is started. It can also be worked using wool as the couched thread and a variety of silks or cottons to tie it down and make the required design. For inspiration look at heraldry, medieval manuscripts and Celtic designs.

Embroidery using real silk

We are fortunate now to be able to buy a better range of real silk threads and, although the stitches used may overlap many techniques, it is useful to mention that miniature embroideries can gain a richness that is quite distinctive. The amounts used will be small, so it is not quite so costly as it may seem, and if you choose a range of colours that appeals to you, these can be used in conjunction with other threads. Designs should enhance the beauty of the silks, such as Persian miniatures, with an impression of rich colour shining through in small defined areas. Subtle

Two embroideries on easels. Silk bird from Siberian design. Silk couching on silk fabric. Size of frame 9 × 7 cm ($3\frac{1}{2}$ × $2\frac{1}{2}$ in.). Jean Brown.

'Japanese landscape' on silk fabric. Straight stitch in machine twist and one strand of stranded cotton. Size of frame 7 × 5.5 cm ($2\frac{3}{4}$ × 2 in.). May Plummer. Frames and easels by Fred Williams.

changes in colour may not be so obvious in miniature pieces, so put the silks side by side in small quantities to see whether shade changes will actually appear. These can be laid out on to the background fabric to suggest what the effect will be. Always use short lengths (not more than 30 cm (12 in.) in the needle, as it tends to catch either in one's nails or on the edge of a frame or fabric. Simple stitchery, such as couching, long and short stitches, straight, split and stem stitch will let the silks speak for themselves. The tops of tiny boxes, really small pictures or a special greetings card can be made even more special by using silk. For a present that expresses something of particular value, inspiration might be gained from the rich colours of a stained glass window, with solid silk shading outlined in black, all contained in a small gold or silver frame.

Embroidery on net, white work and darning

All these techniques lend themselves to small designs and there are many examples in museums which will make us wonder whether our ancestors had more patience and better eyesight than ourselves. Old pieces of net are a joy to work on, being usually made of cotton in square sections, whereas modern nylon net is hexagonal and much more slippery. Yet even tiny pieces of modern curtain nets can be used to advantage, particularly if worked in white or silver and then backed with a contrasting fabric.

For fine darning on net use a sewing thread, one strand of embroidery cotton or fine silk. When starting the work leave an

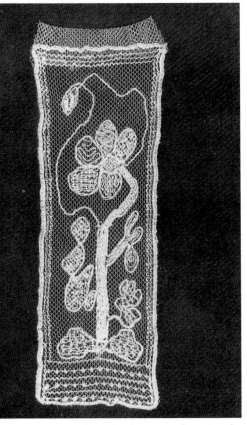

end on the front, and secure the first stitch with a small back stitch into the design. The loose end can be woven neatly into the back of the design if this is to be visible. If the back is not to be visible place a piece of background fabric into the ring frame and mount the embroidery on to this, taking the loose ends through from the front to where they can be secured invisibly into the background fabric.

Darning in ornamental patterns was popular on samplers, and for small designs these can be very effective, worked in bright colours on material such as huckaback or even weave. Use a darning thread which is slightly thicker than the weave of the fabric so that it will not get lost in the weave. Keep pattern areas simple so that the effect of the darning can be seen. A tiny sampler for a dollshouse could be worked this way, or a needlecase could be worked in coarser threads. For this a handwoven wool or a furnishing fabric with an even weave might make a good background contrast to simple darning.

Other kinds of white work, such as Ayrshire and Mountmellick, can be adapted using fine threads, particularly sewing cotton. Look in old embroidery books for these techniques which went out of fashion, and where the traditional ways

ABOVE LEFT
Dollshouse curtain. Hexagonal net. Pattern darning with stranded cotton. 14 × 4.5 cm (5½ × 2 in.).

ABOVE RIGHT
Rose motif. Coarse even weave. Darning in stranded cotton and coton à broder. 8.5 cm (3½ in.) square.

74

of completing them can be found. Keep the designs simple with flower and leaf motifs which can be interpreted in areas of chain, buttonhole, eyelets, bullion and French knots. For transferring the design on to the fabric a tacked or stitched line from the back can be used as part of the finished embroidery.

Patchwork and quilting

It is very satisfying to see miniature patchwork in a dollshouse, for cushions and bedspreads, but there is no reason why the use of small scale patches cannot be adapted for other articles.

Star bedspread for a dollshouse. Small patterned cottons in diamond patchwork. 19 cm (7½ in.) square. Val Anderson.

Traditional patchwork techniques using hexagons, squares, diamonds, etc. are applicable, but obviously the scale of all the materials used has to be adapted. The following list is for guidance when searching for materials for small scale patchwork:
— A good metal template is essential for cutting; these are purchasable as small as 6 mm ($\frac{1}{4}$ in.) or you can cut them *accurately* from card.
— Polycottons in plain and tiny patterned designs are good, but some people prefer to work with pure cotton which can be given a good crease when necessary.
— Papers can be cut from writing paper or thin greetings cards. Some embroiderers prefer to work without a paper. For cutting accurately, graph or isometric paper is very useful as the grid paper provides a cutting guide.
— Needles should be as fine as possible, a number 11 is suitable, and tiny pins which are about half an inch long, known as 'lills'.
— Sewing threads may be too coarse to go in a fine needle and would damage the fabric. Polyester sewing threads are finer and now come in a good range of colours.
— Sharp pencils, a metal edge ruler, sharp paper and embroidery scissors, and a soft board of some kind (such as cork tile for laying out the pieces when the design has been decided upon) are useful.

Accuracy is essential in miniature patchwork as the slightest deviation will show on the finished article. The great advantage, however, is that unlike a full-size bedspread the patches can be spread out for display and the final design chosen without too much difficulty. If they are pinned to a soft board they can be left in position and sewn together as required.

Wadding or padding is not generally required for dollshouse bedspreads as this makes them too stiff, but for cushions a small piece of wadding can be put in. Poke it in after sewing up the cushions, but do not use scissors as they might pierce the fabric.

A backing fabric of similar weight is needed for a bedspread in a toning or contrasting colour. This can be sewn on in one of two ways.

(1) If the backing fabric is to be invisible from the front it can be seamed together on the sewing machine round three sides, turned out the right way and the fourth side slip-stitched into position.

(2) The backing fabric should be cut larger than the size of the finished bedspread and put face down on a flat surface. The bedspread should be laid on this right side up, then the backing can be brought over the front, turned in and slip-stitched neatly into place. Corners can be mitred or two long sides turned over first, followed by the two short sides, making a squared off corner. This method will obviously

*Box lid in small Suffolk
puffs in silk. Diameter
of box lid 6.5 cm
(2½ in.). Mary Roberts.*

cover some of the front design so allowance should be made
for this when planning the patchwork.

Other kinds of patchwork can be adapted for miniature work and
their construction will depend on your being able to find fine
fabrics and manipulate the small pieces. These pieces include
Somerset star, log cabin, Suffolk puffs and Seminole. Cathedral
window in a small scale would be an interesting challenge and the
'stained glass' type of patchwork could be very effective.

Various kinds of patchwork can be simulated extremely well
using ribbon instead of fabric, and these are explained in more
detail in the section on ribbon embroidery.

Quilting

The details of quilting are often lost on a miniature piece as the
fabric provides too much 'bounce' and the stitching is not defined
sufficiently. Back stitches give a better line than the traditional
running stitches, and the quilting will show up more if the fabric
used does not have a shine on the surface. A good quality muslin
might be better for an experiment, therefore, than a cotton or silk.
Wadding between the layers of fabric would be too thick unless
you want to make a really deep eiderdown. An extra layer of
cotton to act as the wadding will generally be sufficient. Tiny

knots can be aded to the surface which can be tied either on the front or back. French knots make an interesting detail, and it is not necessary to do each one separately. After completing the knot, run the needle between the layers of fabric to the next position. Always secure it with tiny back stitches run invisibly into the fabric; take the end out to the side of the work and snip it off with small sharp scissors as close to the fabric as possible.

Ribbon embroidery

In recent years the revival of interest in the use of ribbons for embroidery and even knitting has meant that manufacturers have produced interesting leaflets about their products and many patterned and plain ribbons are available in different widths. Ribbons can be woven, couched down, used for cross stitch or French knots, or for a variety of decorative effects. They are firm, have selvedges and generally do not tend to fray. Their potential for miniature embroidery seems unlimited, and I hope that the suggestions given here are the beginning of experiments that other embroiderers will take up as a fascinating challenge.

Using ribbon as a thread

On an interesting background fabric ribbon can be used for couching down linear patterns, for twisting into scroll patterns, or for putting into the needle to work a variety of stitches. Ribbon stitchery will stand up from its background and give a textured effect so do not make it too fussy or try to combine it with flatter stitches to show off its raised quality. On canvas and other meshes ribbon can be woven in or used for conventional stitches such as half-cross, a full-cross stitch, or any of the straight stitches associated with canvas work. It may tend to twist as it is worked, and this can leave gaps between the ribbon threads showing the canvas underneath. Try a sample stitch to determine whether this happens. In some designs part of the canvas can be left bare anyway so that this will not matter. If bare canvas is not wanted, work in flat stitchery first, or paint the canvas in an appropriate colour with waterproof pencils or dyes. (Tubular ribbons are now available and these can be threaded with wire or a strong sewing cotton and pulled up to make ruching.)

Using ribbon as a fabric

In a successful experiment I discovered that ribbons could be used to make a decorative picture in a very quick method which is useful for miniature embroidery. The complexity of the design can depend entirely on the idea that you want to express and the time you have to execute it. The sample I have shown here is of the simplest kind and is illustrated in colour plate 3. To hold these ribbons in place effectively, the picture needs to be mounted

78

under tension and enclosed in a frame. It could be used for a greetings card if the mount were sufficiently strong. I chose ribbons in my 'store' which expressed the colours of a landscape and decided that the main emphasis of the design was on the horizontals to express the receding view.

Mount a piece of cotton in a ring frame which is large enough for the design plus at least an inch on each of the four sides. The lengths of ribbon need to be long enough to go across the design and over the edge of the backing card so that they will be kept under tension. Work out the design roughly on a piece of paper or work directly from a photo or drawing. Thread two needles with strong sewing thread – the colour is irrelevant as this will not show. Starting at the bottom of the picture, lay the first piece of ribbon and attach it just outside the edge of the design area. This can be marked with pencil on the backing fabric. Secure the other side with the second needleful of thread, making sure that the ribbon is horizontal. Lay each piece of ribbon closely against the previous one until the picture is complete. (I tried sewing into the selvedge of the ribbons to attach them more securely but even this minute stitching showed and I wanted a clear gradation without any obvious stitchery.) Double-sided sticky tape could be fixed to the backing fabric to get extra adhesion for the ribbon, but care must be taken in placing the ribbons correctly.

You can put some decorative stitching on the ribbon to add texture and secure them as well. Then cover the whole picture with a fine white chiffon before putting it on backing card and framing it. Experiments could be made by adding some gauzes to give highlights and by weaving in other ribbons or fabrics, but the essence of such pictures is their simplicity, so beware of adding too much. Iron-on interfacing might also be used on which to attach the ribbons, but test a piece of ribbon first with an iron, or the results might be disastrous.

Ribbons can also be used to simulate patchwork or woven fabric. The Victorians were very fond of woven ribbons for cushions and smaller items, and some of the complicated patterns found in old books might be adapted for making miniature items today. The ribbon can also be combined with tiny patterned fabrics in weaving. If fabrics are used cut them double the width required and iron back the turnings to give a neat, creased finish. The raw edges will not show, being hidden within the weaving. Decide on the size of the finished piece and also the width of ribbon required to make the woven effect. The narrower the ribbon the more complex the design can be. Mount a piece of cotton backing into a ring frame and mark the size of the design on to it. Pin the vertical ribbons and fabrics in the pattern, allowing the smallest possible gap between each one. Make sure all the verticals are straight, then sew the ribbons, top and

bottom, outside the design area to the backing fabric. Taking the horizontal ribbons and fabrics weave these across. When correctly in position sew these at each end as well. The piece can then be finished according to the purpose for which it is intended.

Ribbons can be used in the patchwork called Somerset star, for which squares of fabric are normally folded into rectangles and then into triangles. This prevents raw edges showing in the patchwork. With ribbon this problem does not arise, and the lengths of ribbon need to be only folded into triangles. It is easiest to work with the backing fabric in a ring frame to keep the embroidery under tension. The accompanying diagrams show how to place the first four triangles of ribbon in the centre, and then the succeeding layers. Attach them firmly at the apex of each triangle with the smallest of stitches and also one or two equally small stitches on the outside edge. A continuous thread can be used for this as the work proceeds. The shape of Somerset star patchwork seems to go more readily into a circle, so these can be finished off with a backing and padding if they are wanted as dollshouse cushions. For a picture, needlecase or other flat surface they can be backed as appropriate. If a squared design is wanted, then extra fabric needs to be added at the corners or an extra ribbon triangle placed to create the right shape.

In Seminole patchwork strips of fabric are sewn together and then cut to make decorative patterns which can be laid either vertically or in diagonals, with plain bands of fabric between, often decorated with braids. This can be done with fine cottons, using either hand or machine sewing, and keeping the strips to a very narrow width. Iron them well and cut the turnings back so that they lie neatly underneath. This can also be attempted with ribbons, creating the patterns directly with the ribbons sewn on

ABOVE LEFT
Dollshouse bedspread. Woven strips of cotton and ribbon decorated with French knots and edged with lace. 9 × 7 cm (3½ × 2½ in.).

ABOVE RIGHT
Somerset star cushion in ribbon. Diameter 4.5 cm (1¾ in.).

Diagrams for Somerset star patchwork –

(1) Square of fabric folded into rectangle.

(2) The rectangle folded into a triangle. If ribbon is used this is the first fold necessary.

(3) The four triangles placed together on the centre of the backing fabric. Tacked or drawn lines can be put on the backing fabric of calico or cotton to make sure placing is accurate.

(4) Successive placing of layers of triangles. As the work proceeds eight triangles are needed in a layer to fill the space. Always make sure the outer edges of the previous layer are covered with each succeeding row. On a 10 cm (4 in.) square, using 5 cm (2 in.) squares of fabric or 2.5 cm (1 in.) ribbon, five layers of triangles would be needed.

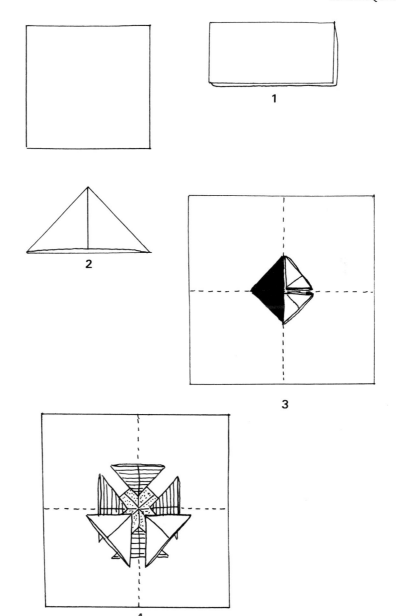

to a background fabric. The bands of the design can be drawn on to the backing fabric for guidance and the lengths of ribbon should be slightly longer than each band and attached firmly at each raw edge. This will then need to be covered with fabric or a wider ribbon and two lots of ribbon design could have their edges covered by one strip in this way. It is important to lay the ribbons as flatly as possible and to make sure they are as close to each other as they can be to prevent the backing fabric showing through.

Log cabin patchwork also uses strips of fabric which are sewn round into a square on a backing fabric, traditionally with one light side and one dark side. The squares are then sewn together to form the overall design. As in Seminole this can be achieved in miniature with the use of fine fabrics, either sewn by hand or on the sewing machine. The use of ribbon closely follows the techniques already described. Use a backing fabric of the appropriate colour as this will form the central square of the log cabin block. Several small blocks can be worked on a ring frame, spaced out and then cut out afterwards. (I used a 3 mm ($\frac{1}{8}$ in.) wide ribbon for my experiment, cutting each tiny piece of ribbon just longer than required for each strip.) As each strip is laid attach each end firmly to the backing fabric and also put one or two stitches in the back selvedge of the ribbon which will not show when the block is finished. As each strip is laid overlap the previous layer of ribbon fractionally to prevent a gap appearing. When all the blocks are completed cut them out with a small amount left for turning on the background fabric. Join them with seams as close to the last strip of ribbon as possible. An alternative would be to leave a fraction of the background fabric showing when the seams are done to make sewing easier and then to add a strip of ribbon between the blocks across the whole area

Pieced dollshouse quilt.
Appliqué cottons.
17 cm (6$\frac{3}{4}$ in.) square.
Val Anderson.

of patchwork. This will neaten the edges between the blocks and make a unifying grid across the whole design.

Techniques where fabrics are applied

Appliqué is often regarded as a quick means of decorating other fabrics and providing instant embroidery. It is also often confused with collage, where materials are glued to the background surface rather than stitched.

Appliqué can be heavy in texture and rather overwhelming,

Cottage garden. Appliqué cottons. Decorative stitchery, cut and uncut velvet stitch for hedges. 14×9 cm ($5\frac{1}{2} \times 3\frac{1}{2}$ in.).

especially when the scale of the total piece is small. The weight of the fabric and its type of weave, texture, etc. must be looked at in relation to the design and any other types of embroidery combined with it. Even a light coloured piece of fabric can dominate because of the weight of the material. Also the question of bulk has to be considered in relation to turnings and seams. A dollshouse cushion for example, can become very unwieldy when it is sewn together. The use of iron-on interfacings, bonding materials and bindings can make edges less prone to fraying, especially when closely woven fabrics are used. Edges can also be finished with a fine couched line, so avoiding the need for turnings. Iron-on interfacings will make fabrics less pliable, so this should be considered when the purpose of the embroidery is decided.

Expensive silks and gauzes can be used very economically on miniature embroidery where only tiny pieces may be needed to highlight a certain area of the design and will not be too heavy in texture. A greetings card can be made with a minimum of extra embroidery if the fabrics have a special quality in themselves. Felt, at the other end of the fabric scale, is useful for padding, but it has a very heavy 'dead' appearance and should be used sparingly on small embroideries.

Shadow quilting is a mixture of appliqué and quilting: coloured fabrics are put under a layer of transparent or semi-opaque materials and their outline quilted. This seems to work very well on a small scale and gives the sense of depth that may be lost from ordinary quilting in miniature. Fabrics can also be

Canvas slip. Fine canvas worked with tent stitch applied to satin. English seventeenth century. 8 cm (3½ in.) square. Private collection.

applied to nets and then cut away in different layers to simulate three dimensional effects. There are many experiments to be made in playing around with layers of fabrics of varying weights and transparency. Simple designs are necessary to heighten the quality of the fabrics.

On some designs needlelace pieces may be suitable for appliqué and can be combined with other stitchery. Fabrics constructed out of knitted and crocheted wool may also be useful if some kind of lacy surface is needed to lighten the design. Canvas work 'slips' are pieces of canvas work which are then cut out and applied to a background fabric. These were extremely popular in the seventeenth century and have the advantage of allowing very small motifs to be worked separately. For a modern miniature embroidery this technique would be equally appropriate, but a fairly fine canvas is needed to prevent the slip becoming too dominating. The edge of the canvas can be neatened with a couched line, and padding can be added under the motif if a slightly raised effect is wanted. From here the technique of appliqué begins to overlap with raised and stump work.

Techniques with fabrics or threads cut away

In this section a whole range of traditional techniques can be included, such as broderie anglaise, drawn thread, hardanger,

Rose motif. Even weave, with drawn ground background. Rose outlined in chain stitch. 7 cm (2¾ in.) square.

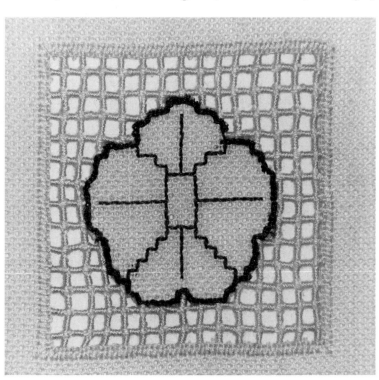

hedebo, drawn grounds and needleweaving. For a small embroidery a simple motif like a flower spray or border pattern may be sufficient. Coarser fabrics, such as hessian or scrim, can be used with a minimum of stitches in either a matching or contrasting thread. If a more lacy pattern is required use a finer thread in a matching colour. If the stitchery is important the colour can be a foil to the background.

If threads are to be cut away the final purpose of the item is helpful in deciding how it can be finished off neatly. If a backing fabric is used the ends can be taken through and secured. For book marks, for which needleweaving is an excellent technique, the ends will have to be darned into the stitchery. Look for border patterns on furniture, stone carvings on church doorways and arches, or on old samplers.

One type of embroidery which overlaps both appliqué and cut work and has become popular again in recent years is characterized by the molas of the San Blas Indians from the islands off Panama. It involves two or more layers of fabric which are cut away in sections to reveal different layers in contrasting colours. If this technique is worked to the high degree of skill shown in the San Blas islands it can qualify as miniature embroidery, for the layers have to be accurately cut and minute turnings sewn down invisibly. With a simple geometric, plant or animal motif it could be used for a small embroidery, perhaps making use of particularly rich and exotic fabrics shown against layers of plain cotton.

Machine embroidery

The use of the machine for embroidery seems to be very much a matter of personal choice, and there are many considerations both for and against it. Some very fine examples of pictures worked in a realistic style have been produced in recent years and, although these might be extremely fiddly to work on a smaller scale, there is no reason why they should not be attempted. However, it is probable that the end result would not necessarily hold any advantage over hand sewing, using basic stitches.

The main advantage for machine embroidery in miniature is that it gives a strength and substance to the fabric and so to the finished piece. This can be exploited in a number of ways. The introduction of water-soluble fabrics, either in cold or boiling water, has added to the exciting possibilities of making 'lace' simulated embroideries, and miniature examples are both satisfying and successful to make. The point to remember is that all lines of stitchery on the soluble fabric must be attached at some point to another line of thread or the design will fall apart when the fabric is dissolved. The design can be pencilled on to the soluble fabric. Work a straight stitch over the main lines of the

Tree worked on hot water soluble fabric with machine embroidery cotton, using straight and zigzag stitches. 15 × 12.5 cm (6½ × 5 in.). Lily Waldron.

design first, then add to this with zig-zag, straight and any other machine stitches in the colours required. After the fabric has been dissolved according to manufacturers' instructions, lay the piece out flat to dry, stretching it carefully into shape. The tree which is illustrated was actually worked as a sample for a larger panel but was so successful that it has been used on its own.

In making the fabric stronger by heavy machining, many items can be made which will be rigid enough to be cut away afterwards. This stronger fabric is useful for making jewellery, mobiles, Christmas decorations or even small toys. Applied fabrics can be added in rich profusion, in different layers, held down by rows of machine stitching in random or deliberate patterns. Collars, necklaces and key ring attachments are items on which interesting experiments can be made. Sewing machine threads with varying colours, including metallic shades, can be used on plain backgrounds, but beware making the machine embroidery so heavy that it becomes a mess and loses the impact of the design. Stained glass window patterns can be achieved with the use of dark outlining of bright areas, the latter being worked either in stitchery or appliqué.

Many modern machines have a variety of stitches which can be exploited for miniature embroideries. Simple border patterns can be worked for book marks, cards, etc. and a variety of threads used in the top or bottom spools. Couch down thicker threads using random doodle designs to make a quickly executed greetings card. Quick 'doodling' samples made with a variety of threads using a minimum of stitchery – but on an interesting background fabric – may produce some unexpected results, one or two of which may be worth pursuing further as ideas.

The sewing machine is ideal for creating shadow quilting where layers of fabric can be applied and sewn down in areas of design. Appliqué pieces can also be securely fastened with the machine but left with edges unattached to give a slightly raised effect. For this use fabrics which will not fray, or try singeing the edges before attaching them to the background fabric. Make sure ends are well secured so the sewing does not come undone.

The sewing machine is also invaluable for miniature embroidery for simulating other techniques. With the smallest stitch width and length and working on muslin, it is possible to imitate Ayrshire, as was done on the dollshouse christening gowns illustrated. For the gowns I first used real silk in the bottom spool but found that this did not show up as silk and instead used a fine

Dollshouse christening gowns. Muslin. Machine embroidery in silk and fine embroidery thread. Each garment is 6.5 cm (2½ in.) in length. The shawl worked by the same method is 16 cm (6½ in.) square.

cotton in both spools. The most difficult part was constructing the gowns, but certainly imitation white work for dollshouse or doll accessories can be successful using this method. Lines of straight stitching could also be used to simulate fine couching and fine metallic threads would provide tiny gleams of colour.

When working on the machine on miniature embroidery tidy up the ends of threads as you proceed with the work. A tangle of ends left on the back can spoil the piece and may be pulled through accidentally to the front. The use of a ring frame obviously makes this easier and the machine can be used with the teeth feed either up as in ordinary sewing or down as for free embroidery. With the range of threads available for use on the sewing machine today experiments in miniature offer great possibilities.

Raised embroidery and stump work

One of the exciting characteristics of embroidery is that it can cover a complete range, from work which is as flat as the weave of the background fabric through highly textured pieces to free standing soft sculpture. In this section I shall concentrate on

Needlelace motifs based on slices of agate. Metallic threads and silk. Each one is approximately 5 cm (2 in.) long. Flowers of silk threads worked in buttonhole stitch for petals and leaves, with wrapped stems. Maximum length 11 cm (4½ in.). Lily Waldron.

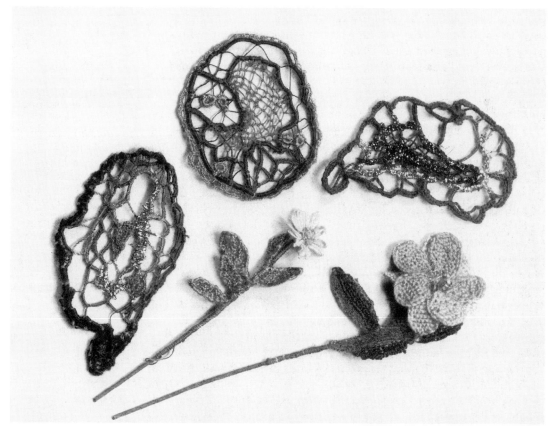

miniature embroideries that stand between 'flat' stitchery and three dimensional pieces. The urge to touch the beautiful textured items that are displayed in exhibitions is often strong. In creating these in miniature we can perhaps allow ourselves and other people to enjoy that sensation.

Many of the relevant embroidery stitches come from the work we know as raised or stump work. The boxes, mirror surrounds and other objects so popular in the seventeenth century give us tiny details of costume, hair, faces and hands and architecture in raised embroidery. Needlelace stitches, such as detached buttonhole, can be worked in a variety of threads and can be as dense or as open as required for the design. Layers can be built up with detached areas of stitches, or padding used of felt or leather to increase the raised effect. Trees and leaves are particularly suitable as the shapes and texture can be worked with quite intricate detail. A crisp finish is vital if the right scale is to be maintained, or the applied pieces will be too heavy and mar the design.

For modern raised work it is helpful to consider the whole range of nets and meshes that can be obtained cheaply. Vegetable and fruit bags come in a variety of colours, do not fray, can be cut easily and are highly adaptable. Some are more rigid and can be used for walls or garden fences. Metal meshes, and even nylon garden meshes may make a 'trellis' for a small embroidery. At Christmas treat yourself to some chocolate money and then keep the fine gold bags it is packed it.

Discarded objects are also ideal for use in miniature raised embroideries. The extensive use of mixed media techniques has also liberated embroiderers. Paper, often home made, wood or metal can now be used in designs which need that special textural quality which cannot be found in fabric and threads.

Insertion and smocking are two techniques which might also be used to give raised effects in miniature. Insertions in fine threads could add interesting decorative detail. Although the stitches are basically linear, they could be developed for experiments in rock formations, tree trunks or the lines of fields in a landscape. Books on embroidery give instructions on how to work the insertion stitches and generally suggest the two adjoining fabrics are tacked on to stiff paper to hold them under proper tension. Interfacing fabric could be used as a substitute or even a contrasting backing fabric which is left in when the embroidery is finished. A greetings card could consist of patterned fabrics joined by an insertion stitch with a plain contrasting fabric behind it. This would be unusual and economical in time and cost.

The choice of fabric for smocking is crucial as it must pleat evenly and in tiny folds, yet the smocking on top of it must be

Muslim city. Three variations of smocking on cotton and rayon fabrics. 15.5 × 14.5 cm (6 × 5¾ in.).

visible and add to the design. Because the pleats have some depth I think this technique could be explored for use with raised embroidery. Islamic architecture with its geometric forms or the decoration on a timber framed building might work well in a smocked surface. With more free smocking there are possibilities of interpreting tree bark, fungal growths or wave formations where not all the pleats are taken uniformly into the top stitchery.

Beads

Beadwork was much favoured by the Victorians and earlier generations for use on panels, small purses, cushions, etc. Beadwork was combined with other types of embroidery, particularly with Berlin wool work on canvas. In other cultures, too, fine beading has been used, and many of the native peoples of North America created beautiful bead designs. Beadwork gives an interesting raised texture to small embroideries, but must be used sparingly. There is no doubt that they can give a highlight where a change of texture or reflected light is important.

Beads can be sewn on separately with a fine beading needle or threaded on to a waxed thread. This could then be put into a needle for sewing down or the line of beads can be couched down with another thread. Linear and curved designs can be created

this way when it might be difficult to sew the beads on individually and still get a smooth line.

It is also useful to understand the very old craft of making beads from paper and fabric. For paper beads take a triangle of paper and roll it tightly round a cocktail stick, securing the final layer with glue. The glossy coloured paper from magazines makes beautiful beads this way, and the beads can be varnished for extra protection. Once the cocktail stick is taken out they can be attached to embroideries or made into earrings or jewellery. Felt beads can also be made by rolling rectangles of fabric up and then sewing or gluing them; you can add decorative stitching if required.

Three dimensional embroidery

There is a wide range of embroidery that can be made in a three dimensional form, from the completely practical to the purely decorative. Construction and finishing are vitally important when planning such a piece and will depend on the actual type of embroidery and its final purpose. For this reason this section has been divided into different types of three dimensional projects. Most of these will overlap the techniques that have already been described.

Two-sided embroideries

These are items which are likely to be handled a great deal and include bookmarks, mobiles with flat pieces, jewellery, Christmas decorations and gift tags. They can be worked with stitchery which is two-sided in itself, they can consist of two layers of embroidery joined together or they can be backed with fabric. What puts them together in one category is that each side will be given equal prominence.

ABOVE LEFT
Beads made from rolled paper and felt. Sizes from 1–3 cm (approximately ½–1¼ in.). Nancy McGuinness.

ABOVE RIGHT
Bead pictures, glued and sewn on even weave fabric. Each one is 4.5 cm (1¾ in.) in diameter. May Plummer.

Samples of three dimensional embroidery inspired by Japanese designs. Silk with silk stitchery, padded and corded. 11 × 6 cm (4½ × 2½ in.). Marlene Little.

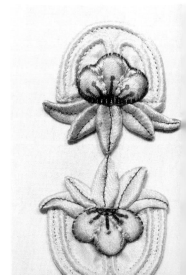

Embroidered jewellery is often most successful when it does not try to imitate precious metal, but exploits the use of fabric and thread. Many of the techniques already mentioned could be used, but bear in mind that edges have to be neatened without being clumsy, that the jewellery needs some weight of its own if it is to hang properly, and that the effect must make an impact from a distance as well as close up.

Embroidered Christmas decorations and small motifs for mobiles are often used as sources for competition ideas, and it is fun to experiment with the many techniques that are suitable. I find that canvas is an ideal fabric for working such pieces. When working a Norwich stitch (or Southern cross) one day for a Christmas decoration I tried to find a way that would make it both flat and decorative on the back. One of these is given here and was one of the unexpected pleasures of experimentation.

Diagram for reversible Norwich stitch.
(TOP) this shows the 'front' of the stitch as it usually appears when worked. It can be worked over any number of odd threads. Note: the thread comes from the back to the front on the odd numbers and goes down into the canvas from front to back on the even numbers.
(BOTTOM) this shows the reverse of the stitch, giving a woven effect. Note that the lower lines are not absolutely horizontal. The last thread marked with a zig-zag line can be taken over the top or threaded into the centre of the stitch. This variation was discovered accidentally by Margaret Hathaway Tibbs, further worked on by Joan Botteley and finally mastered by the author!

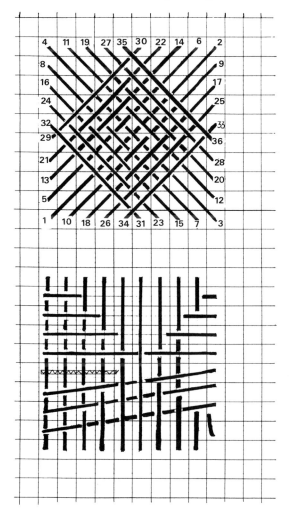

93

Kinetic embroidery

This is a style of embroidery which I think is still to be explored. Kinetic art, which involves movement, has been prominent in art history in this century. In miniature embroidery this can include toys for children, especially advent calendars, 'executive toys' such as puzzles and sets of noughts and crosses, or hangings where selected pieces of the design can be changed around. Many of the items, therefore, will be two-sided pieces, but some may be three-dimensional.

The surface of the fabric used is crucial in determining what kind of movement is required. Two felt-like surfaces will adhere to one another, and so pictures can be made for children where sections can be moved around. A small picture of a house could have the exterior on one side and the interior on the other. Slippery surfaces will be ideal if a sliding process is involved, as in moving woven strips sideways. Adhesive fabrics can be used to hold pieces on, but once removed, the strip left will show. Small hooks and eyes work well and are neat for hanging the 24 pieces for an advent calendar. Buttons can also be used. If pieces are hung on cords, do not use a thread that will stretch or the effect may be spoiled over a period of time.

Decorative foliage for garden scenes can be worked in many ways, with techniques already described, such as the soluble fabrics. The embroidery can then be wired to hang or be sewn into position. Machine sewing is ideal for making such small items as they are strong and can be cut to make a firm, neat edge. Net makes a good foundation for leaves and flowers on to which threads can be sewn down in the shapes and colours desired, then cut and wired so that they can be freestanding. These are also flexible enough to be moved to give variations in the embroidery.

Boxes and cubes

Small boxes are always popular and the interest of the embroidery can be both on the outside and on the linings or surprise interiors. It is not always easier to use a box that has already been constructed, but old boxes can be put to good use. These can become a feature in their own right if you can think of a related design idea that would use the best qualities of the box. An old cigarette box that opened up to reveal a rack of three layers of cigarettes was changed into a model of a box at the races where fashionable miniature ladies were seen in the stands. Boxes with suitable compartments can be made into small dollshouses or receptacles for small treasures. An old sewing box could be used to make a sampler of different techniques in miniature. A decorated box could contain family photographs and records with the house and garden depicted. Keep any such box out

Single Suffolk puff on box lid in silk. Box lid 6.5 cm (2½ in.) in diameter. Mary Roberts.

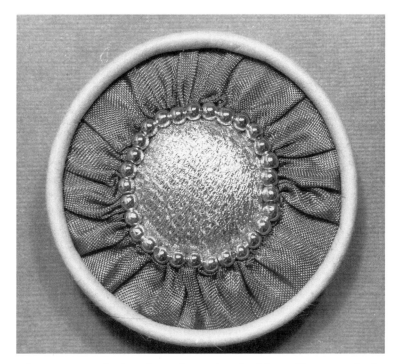

where you can look at it, and one day the idea will emerge for its new embroidered contents.

Decorative cubes can be made which do not have the construction problems of opening lids and hinges. These can be adapted to make interesting textured toys with inert substances such as beads inside to give an intriguing sound as well when shaken. Beads and threads on wire could be hung in open-sided cubes. A three dimensional landscape is possible, showing rocks or caves inside the cubes.

Sculptural embroidery

Embroidery has always had a sculptural element, but fashions change and this aspect has often been neglected. With the interest in multi-media art in recent years more emphasis has been placed on this kind of embroidery and it opens up possibilities in miniature as well as in larger pieces. Pincushions can take many shapes and become small embroidered sculptures. The box of sweets illustrated on the back jacket was originally designed for this purpose. One problem in the construction of such pieces is to make the base heavy enough, so they either need to be mounted on a base such as pottery or weighted with lead, or sand. Make sure any such weights are wrapped securely in plastic then in fabric so that no marks will come through to spoil the embroidery.

Many items for dolls and dollshouses call for sculptural and

three-dimensional elements. There is great scope here for the embroiderer who wants to experiment with soft furnishings on a small scale. Beds, sofas and chairs can be copied from earlier periods of history and made as accurate as possible in their style and colour of embroidery.

The garden bowl illustrated here is a beautiful example of miniature techniques combined. The flowers, canvas work base, pile hedge and wrapped wire trees and trellis are superb pieces of embroidery in their own right. It is satisfying to see the bowl as a whole piece of sculpture, but one's eye is also drawn to the detail as well. Gardens provide a constant source of inspiration and are immensely satisfying when portrayed in three dimensions. Dollshouses in fabric can also be charming; the one illustrated in colour plate 2 is 17 cm wide × 19 cm high (7 × 7½ in.) and was worked on canvas and decorated with beads. It was made as a silver wedding present and has a furnished interior as well.

Garden bowl. Bowl woven in basketry techniques in wool. Base of tent stitch with raised hedge on canvas. Textured flowers in wool, ribbon, pearl threads and beads. Tree on wire with machine embroidered leaves. Wire archway wrapped in thread. Door machine embroidered. Overall diameter 23 cm (9¼ in.) and 7.5 cm (3 in.) deep. Margaret Hathaway Tibbs.

8 Construction

When working in miniature, it is often the construction of the final piece that poses the most problems. Wherever possible think the stages through first, if necessary making rough samples in similar fabrics or materials, or even in paper and thin card, to see what problems may occur. Even so, it is the constant challenge of embroidery that guarantees a tricky situation may happen just when least expected.

Gluing or sewing
This seems to be a matter of personal preference, but one or other technique may be more suitable for particular items. Glue may not always provide sufficient tension for a small piece that has to be stretched tightly. Careful sewing can usually be unpicked if necessary, whereas glue may leave a permanent mark on the fabric even if it can be pulled apart.

Two- or three-fold greetings cards can be fixed most easily using a minimum of white PVA glue. Place the embroidery when ready for mounting on a cork tile, or any material that is clean and will take pins, face upwards. Do a trial placement of the card over the embroidery and mark the corners of the visible section with pins placed vertically into the embroidery. Lift the card off carefully leaving the pins in position. Glue the back of the card and place it straight down on the embroidery using the pins as corner markers. Do not put the glue too near the inner edges of the card or it may run towards the embroidery. Double-sided sticky tape may also be used as an adhesive by the same method.

Hand or sewing machine
In intricate pieces where many corners are required it is often easier to get a short needle into the corner and secure firmly with small back stitches than to try to manoeuvre the sewing machine. But if the embroidery is to be handled a great deal the added strength of machine-made seams may be preferred. Remember that even machine stitching can come undone and ends should be firmly secured if there is to be any strain on the seam. Decorative

machine sewing is a technique in itself, but sometimes the use of embroidery stitches on the machine can be both part of the construction and the design.

Boxes

Many small items depend on a box-type construction, and there are books dealing with the necessary techniques involved. In miniature pieces there are the added considerations of limited space for working, seams needing to be fine enough not to spoil the dimensions and the thickness of fabric being more crucial. Do not be mean with fabric and always leave a larger working area which can be cut away when the box is constructed. If possible, experiment with the fabric, stretching it to test its strength, its opaqueness and its thickness.

Some of the basics for working in miniature are as follows.
— It is easier to have as few seams as possible, so cut the outer card for the box to include all four sides, leaving only two sides to be joined. The base can also be cut out of the same piece, but it is better to have a separate lid which will be attached with fabric hinges or stitchery.
— Thin card, such as the sort used for cereal boxes, is adequate for small boxes, one thickness to be used for the outer box and one for the lining. This, together with the fabric, will produce quite a strong box if its overall dimensions are not more than 10 cm (4 in.).
— Lining fabric is usually finer than that used on the outside, unless a particular texture is required inside. Cotton and polycottons are good because they are fine enough to attach to the lining card, but it is not so easy to hide stitches in them. Use a patterned fabric, and the stitches will not be so obvious.
— The shape of the box depends on its final use and many variations exist. Remember that when covered with fabric, the dimensions of the box will be greater than just the card alone, and the added fabric thickness on all sides of the box will affect the

Dollshouse folding bed seat. Constructed from cotton, foam padding, with woven ribbon top. Folded – 5.5 cm square × 4.5 cm (2¼ × 1½ in.) deep.

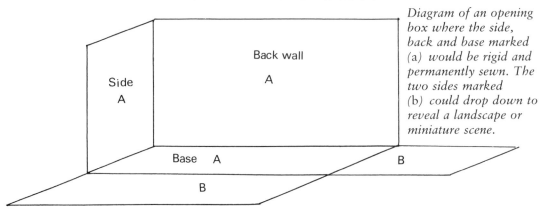

Diagram of an opening box where the side, back and base marked (a) would be rigid and permanently sewn. The two sides marked (b) could drop down to reveal a landscape or miniature scene.

size of the lid. One particular kind of box is attractive for miniature scenes: its lid is completely loose and holds the box together when closed. Two of the sides remain rigid and vertical while the other two adjoining sides come down to form part of the setting. It is also possible to make the lid as a fixed part of the box to form a ceiling, and the two sides which are free to move are attached to the top with bows, or a button and loop. These boxes are ideal for displaying furniture or garden scenes. If carefully thought out in advance the items can be fixed permanently inside so that they do not touch one another but will be in position when the box is opened.

— Sewing up the box can often best be done with a circular needle. Put the wrong sides of the sections together and sew small neat stitches with the circular needle on the right side. When the sections are opened to form the box these stitches will disappear into the angle created. Always ensure that the thread is securely fastened with small backstitches and not just with a knot. If you use a straight needle then slight imperfections can be hidden with a decorative stitch on top, but make sure that the decorative stitching is part of the design and does not look like an afterthought! The best stitch for using with a straight needle is ladder stitch. Place the back sides of the section together and use a strong thread which matches the fabric. As you work, pull on the thread to tighten the stitches a little; this process can be repeated at the end of the section before you fasten off securely. The stitches will disappear into the fabric and make a very neat finish.

Diagram for ladder stitch. The straight stitches go at right angles to the two sections to be joined, with the thread passing inside the folds of the fabric between each straight stitch.

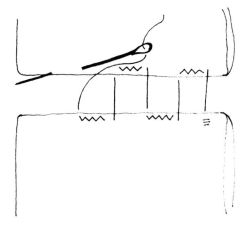

Construction of other articles

Some particular aspects of this section are dealt with in more detail under finishing and framing as many miniature embroideries are basically two-dimensional. The following section deals with general hints on construction.

- Use strong threads, the smallest needles possible, and tiny stitches for neatness and strength.
- If the sewing machine is used for seams, particularly on canvas with geometric designs, accuracy of the seam is essential or the design may be spoilt. Sew a tacking line in the same colour first to hold the two sections together; this need not then be taken out afterwards as the machine stitching will cover it.
- On items such as needlecases, spectacle or scissor cases, belts and other pieces that are to be folded over it is often easier to work out the total design on one piece of fabric or canvas leaving a space unworked where the fold will be. Construction may then be finished in one of two ways.
  (a)   Work a suitable stitch on the unworked fabric that will fold evenly. For this, stitches which go across the fold or cross diagonally will be more satisfactory.
  (b)   Fold the fabric and work a stitch such as long-legged cross which will cover the edge and give a firm finish.
  Either of these methods ensures that the design of the two sides will not be harmed by the folded edge and will make a neat 'frame'.

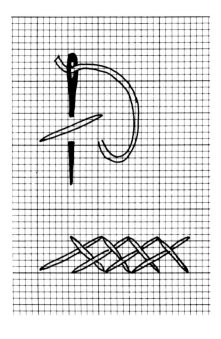

Diagram for long legged cross stitch. To get the right effect the number of threads counted horizontally should be twice the number of threads counted vertically. In this diagram there are ten threads counted from left to right and five threads from top to bottom.

- On some small items it may be difficult to sew seams on the wrong side and then turn them. If this appears likely make sure the stitching that will cover the seam is decorative and strong. Linings are usually thinner and can be made up in the usual way and slipped inside. At the corners or particular points one or two tiny stitches with a matching sewing cotton will secure lining invisibly. Where the lining has to be joined, a slip stitch is often most suitable.

Other useful accessories

Double-sided sticky tape and masking tape are useful for holding fabrics and card down temporarily. Ordinary transparent sticky tape can leave a mark on thin fabric or paper after some time (within a few years), so the discoloration may spoil an embroidery if this is not taken into account.

When working on canvas masking tape protects the edges and prevents finger nails from being caught in the canvas or the working threads. It can easily be pulled off after the embroidery is finished and before the article is made up.

To mop up spare glue thin card or fabric is often better than a paper towel, which tends to stick to everything.

9 Finishing and framing

It is often very disappointing to visit an exhibition of well designed and executed embroidery and find that the finishing and mounting has been carried out in such a manner that the value of the whole is diminished. Professional mounting and framing is expensive but with miniature work much can be done by the embroiderer.

There are various stages in the finishing process and ideally these should be considered before the embroidery is begun, in conjunction with the original design. Different types of finishing are as follows:

- Making up of boxes and cubes (dealt with in the previous section);
- Mounting embroidery behind card (either on greetings cards or on ready made picture frames);
- Mounting embroidery rigidly with a fabric or embroidered frame;
- Making small free standing sculptures, three-dimensional embroideries, or two-sided items.

General notes on finishing and framing
- Keep craft knives sharp, all card for mounting and backing clean and unbent. Keep small pieces of card that may come in useful.
- Keep a piece of hardboard with the smooth side for a clean working surface.
- If possible design your embroidery with the frame or mount in front of you. This will avoid the problem of awkward sizes when the work is finished and give a unity to the project.

Frames
Many small frames are now available from gift shops, stationers and model shops which are ideal for miniature embroideries. If the embroidery is very delicate it may be preferable to retain the

A selection of miniature frames, including key ring holders, jewellery findings, buttons and small rings.

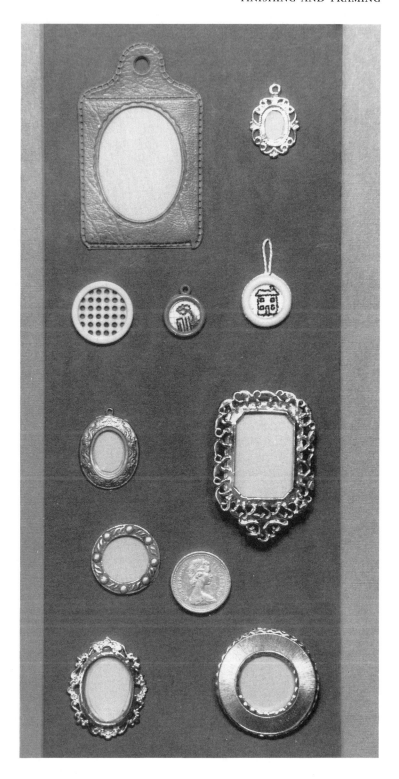

glass or plastic for protection but wherever possible it is better to see the techniques without protection. Glass has a deadening effect on the texture of the stitches, especially non-reflective glass. The quality of miniature work can be spoilt if it cannot be seen in detail. With many of the really tiny frames the embroidery will have to be mounted on very thin card, with glue used to attach it to the card and then another layer of thin card to cover the back. Because there will be very little weight a hanging hook of a strong thread, such as a coton à broder in a matching colour can be fixed between the two layers of card.

Some of the types of frames readily available are as follows.

- Tiny photograph frames, made of brass, silver, wood or plastic, with usually a back in the same material, made either for hanging or standing.
- Plastic and wooden rings of all sizes.

Landscape. Appliqué chiffon and silk scarves with straight stitchery in wool. The frame of plastic mesh was used for part of the design and also embroidered in straight stitch in wool. 17 × 13 cm (7 × 5 in.).

- Buttons with flat centres: if these are used the embroidery will have to be glued to thin card, then glued on to the centre of the button.
- Plastic mesh 'canvas' is ideal for framing as it can be cut to any size. The mount round the embroidery can either be left plain with matching fabric or card behind it or be embroidered. The back will have to be neatened off with card or fabric. Ordinary canvas can also be used in this way.
- Perforated paper that the Victorians used for cards and bookmarks is now available and this can also be cut to make a frame, although this will be more fragile than canvas.
- Small plastic or leather wallets can be used, and these come in a variety of sizes from key rings upwards.
- Plastic photograph frames come either as cubes or as a rigid stand-up frame. It may be difficult to get the fabric between the layers of plastic but it can be done if the embroidery is worked or mounted on a fairly rigid backing. This is also an interesting way of displaying embroideries that are two sided or are transparent in some way. Pulled work, embroidery on gauze or needlelace would be possibilities.
- Plastic double glazing material can be used as a frame, with the embroidery hung either behind or in front of the plastic. Holes can be drilled through the plastic to hang the embroidery and also to provide a hook. Use a hand drill, drilling with a steady motion. If it is too fast the plastic will overheat, if too slow it may splinter, so practise on a spare piece.

Card mounts

Stretching embroideries over card

The card must be thick enough so that under tension it does not bend. Hardboard is preferable, and some specialist shops provide a thinner variety, but even this may be too thick for a small piece. Do not cut away any surplus fabric until the position of the embroidery is quite correct. Always ensure that the work can be laid face down on a clean piece of cloth or board.

(1) Make sure that both fabric and card will fit inside the frame if one is being used.

(2) Cut the backing card accurately; a good way of checking is to measure the two diagonals which should be the same.

(3) As a guideline place the card down on the back of the embroidery and get its position right. The corners of the card can be marked on the embroidery either with pins or, if suitable, a pencil.

(4) Glue or masking tape can be used to hold the embroidery in place on the back of the card, but this means that it is more difficult to change if the position is wrong. If this method is used, mitre the corners of the fabric and make sure the back is as neat and flat as possible.

(5) Lacing with thread to hold the embroidery on the backing card is the best method and can be adjusted afterwards. When both sides are laced, neaten the corners of the fabric by making a mitre; do not cut away any surplus fabric until you are sure the embroidery is correctly positioned.

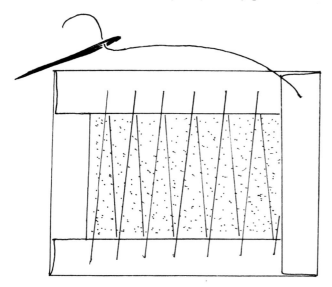

Diagram for lacing fabric over card mounts. Turn over long sides and using strong thread, securely fastened with small back stitches lace across the back as shown. Gently but firmly pull these threads tight and fasten. Then fold over the short sides (one is shown folded over in diagram) and repeat the process.

(6) If the embroidery is not to be placed in another frame, the back can be neatened with thick card, a piece of felt or fabric glued or sewn on. A small loop for hanging the picture can be sewn or taken through this final backing before it is glued or sewn into place. If canvas has been used for the embroidery, remember that the bare canvas will show on the edge of the backing card; work a few extra rows of half-cross stitch to make a neat edge.

Card window mounts

When using a bought frame a card mount can be cut easily and this will improve the appearance of the embroidery. The accompanying diagrams show how to cut a window mount, which can also be used for making greetings cards. A three-fold card will finish the embroidery more neatly and make it more rigid for standing.

Making a window mount

(1) Cut the card to the required size and lay it face down on a clean board. Draw the centre vertical and horizontal lines in pencil. From this the position of the window can be worked out neatly and a decision made as to whether it is going to be central or to one side. Remember that the card window will be reversed when the embroidery is looked at from the right side, so if a window is cut on the right hand side of the back it will appear on the left hand side on the front.

Constructing a frame in fabric – top to bottom).

(1) *Laying the card on the wrong side of the fabric, with pins in corners and sides marked with pencil or chalk.*

(2) *Wrong side of fabric, with card removed, corners strengthened with iron-on interfacing, and cutting of fabric in 'window' area.*

(3) *Card placed back in position, with all four sides cut to required amount, and two of these glued on to the card.*

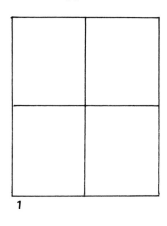

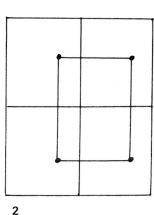

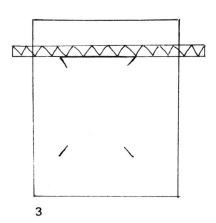

(2) Using the vertical and horizontal lines as a guide, draw the size of the window to be cut on the back of the card and into each corner stick one pin so that it projects through to the right side.

(3) Turn the card on to its right side so the four pins project up. Lay a steel rule against the pins on the outer side and cut firmly from one corner to the other. Do not attempt to cut right into the second corner, but work carefully back from it.

Work this way round all four sides until the card is scored through and the 'window' will fall out. The advantage of this method is that the steel rule protects the frame – if the knife slips it will go into the window section of the mount.

(4) With an oval, circle or irregular window shape draw the shape on the back of the mounting card as before. Then draw an identical shape on a piece of clean card, and cut out the window area with a knife. Put four pins through the mounting card as before and turn on to its right side. Put the spare card on top, using the pins to help position it. Although the edge will not be as firm or as accurate as a steel rule, the top card will protect the mounting card and provide some guide for cutting. The knife should be used in short cutting movements so that it moves regularly round the required shape.

Constructing a frame out of fabric

Fabric mounts, either in the same background material or a different one, work well with miniature embroideries as the weight of the fabric can be matched with the scale and technique of the embroidery.

Using the same background fabric for the frame

(1) Before starting the embroidery make sure the fabric is large enough to provide the frame as well. Put this into a ring frame which is sufficiently large for the design and the frame area so that the fabric will not be unduly marked.

(2) Mark the design area at the edges with a tacking thread and cover the frame area with cloth or tissue paper.

(3) Once the embroidery is finished delineate the frame area with couching or stitchery or by leaving it plain. If padding is required, add a piece of cotton or muslin to the back of the embroidery and do a neat back or decorative stitch through the two layers round the edge of the design. The padding can then be added beneath the frame.

(4) Cut the backing card precisely to the size of the frame, so that the whole piece of fabric can be laced across the back and finished neatly with card or other fabric.

(5) Canvas used in this way can be left plain or embroidered. A much brighter colour fabric can be put between the canvas and the backing card as the canvas will reduce the intensity of colour. Lace the canvas across the back of the card and neaten as with other fabric frames.

Using a different fabric to make a frame
It is possible to attach a fabric frame while the embroidery is still held rigid. This can be done using strips of fabric round the edges or cutting a window. However, this method does tend to lead to puckering of the fabric frame, and turnings can show through unless disguised with padding or card. This method can be used with a more rigid material such as canvas, which can be cut back neatly to provide a window for the embroidery.

It is generally more successful to make a separate frame mounted over card, which is then placed over the embroidery, just as a wooden frame would be attached. With miniature embroideries avoid fussy fabrics or those with textures which will dominate the embroidery too much. Useful steps in the process are as follows:

(*1*) Cut the backing card to the required size and from this cut out the 'visible' area where the embroidery is to show. (See *Making a window mount*, p. 107).

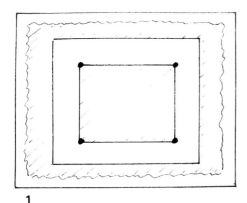

1

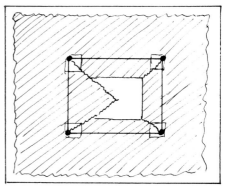

2

Construction of card mounts –
(1) *Marking of centre vertical and horizontal lines on back of card*
(2) *Marking of 'window' area on back of card, with pins placed vertically through card in each corner*
(3) *Front side of card with pins projecting through and ruler placed against pins for cutting.*

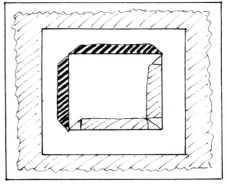

3

(2) Lay the fabric face down on a soft cork or polystyrene tile and place the card frame over it. Mark the corners of the picture area with a pin and draw along the four sides close to the card with a marking pen or tailor's chalk, depending on the colour of the fabric. Remove the card from the fabric, carefully leaving the pins in position.

(3) The corners of the fabric can be strengthened at this stage with a tiny square of iron-on interfacing. Cut out the centre of the fabric, cutting diagonally into the corners but cutting just short of the pins. Cut excess fabric from these four triangular strips but always leave at least a centimetre or half an inch (preferably more) to glue on to the card.

(4) Place the card again in position over the fabric and glue the card. Then pull over the raw edges of fabric on to the card making a neat edge round the picture area. Do not pull too hard or the corners may become torn.

(5) When this is dry this may be placed over the embroidery which has already been mounted on card. The edges of the framing fabric can then be laced or glued across the back and neatened.

Finishing two-sided embroideries

Some examples of miniature embroidery need to be finished neatly on both sides. These will include –

- jewellery, Christmas decorations, mobiles, etc.
- insides of needlecases, bottom of dollshouse carpets
- pincushions, bases of small soft sculptures, dollshouse cushions, etc.

Strength and rigidity can be added by using card, interfacing fabrics, felt or padding. The use of glue or sewing depends on personal preference and the type of fabric being used.

For neat backings, felt or iron-on interfacings can be used, attached with glue or stitchery. Beware of edges that are not absolutely straight as these will show up on a miniature piece. Measure accurately with a ruler and cut precisely with good sharp scissors. Irregularities in stitching tend to show up easily on felt, so sew with a good sharp needle, making tiny stitches wherever possible.

When holding two surfaces together pins sometimes distort the shape. It is easier to take a length of thread in a distinctive colour and take it straight through the backing and the embroidery with a fine, sharp needle, bringing it out again at the same point like a tacking thread. If not pulled tightly it can easily be withdrawn once the two pieces have been joined.

Canvas can be used for a backing and the edges left unworked. Sew together with a double running stitch, making sure the holes

Christmas decoration. Chocolate box fabric with knitted metallic thread, braid and French knots. 9.5 cm × 8 cm (4 × 3 in.).

Small cushions suitable for 'teenage dolls'. Blackwork and Assisi techniques on even weave. Stitchery on blue cotton. Each one is 4 cm (1¾ in.) square.

are correctly positioned to get neat lines of stitches. Leave the canvas larger than necessary before sewing together – it can then be trimmed back to two threads beyond the line of stitching.

It is sometimes preferable to mount both the front and the back of the embroidery on separate pieces of card and attach them to give greater rigidity. They can be joined invisibly with ladder stitch or with a decorative top stitch such as long-legged cross, buttonhole or herringbone. If a small loop is needed for hanging the piece, leave a loop of thread at one corner or in a suitable place while the embroidery is being worked, securing the loop with a couple of back stitches so that it won't slip.

10 Larger embroideries incorporating miniature techniques

Although miniature items are the focus of this book, there are occasions when miniature embroidery can be included in much larger pieces. There are many possible examples such as bedspreads, cushions, play items for children, hangings and three-dimensional items. You could make a pedlar doll, for instance, with a tray of wares made entirely from miniature embroidered items. There will obviously be different priorities to be met when considering the size and impact of the larger piece as a whole and within the design the miniature aspects have to be looked at in their own right.

Sampler for Eleanor. Panel incorporating a variety of miniature embroidery techniques. Size of complete panel – 57.5 × 42.5 cm (23 × 17 in.).

One of the most interesting ways of using miniature techniques is to combine them in a sampler. It seems a pity that so many samplers worked today are still copies of Victorian ideas. The use of a particular theme or a new way of looking at different techniques will give quite a challenging perspective to the sampler. It is also a very enjoyable way of trying out miniature samples. My daughter, Eleanor, wanted a room interior for her sampler which gave me plenty of scope. The following elements were included into the sampler, which was embroidered on an evenweave fabric:

Details for 'Sampler for Eleanor'.

- the carpet (darning and Turkey stitch for the textured pile);
- the clock (pulled work and a bead);
- the architectural details (stem stitch and herringbone);
- small book (cross stitch and Assisi on an interfacing fabric);
- sampler (variety of stitches on 22 canvas);
- lampshade (detached buttonhole on a padded base);
- teddy bear (made of felt as a small stuffed toy);
- bed (made of card covered with plain fabric for head and foot, with a quilted bedspread of patterned cotton);
- the dollshouse (worked on an evenweave linen, with a separate roof);
- small doll (a stump work three-dimensional figure in a smocked dress);
- paintbox and paper (paint and stitchery on interfacing);
- cushions (quilted);
- the figure at the window (made by Rita Green and is stump work with a dress, tiny socks and hair).

There are many scenes or ideas that could be depicted this way, either in realistic or abstract terms. A shop, an art gallery, a family gathering, a house or garden, a collection of stamps – just a few ideas that come to mind. An overall colour scheme is essential but the choice of techniques for the sampler can be made as obvious or as subtle as required. As with other appliqué, the

The fabric shop. Window and front of shop. Lily Waldron

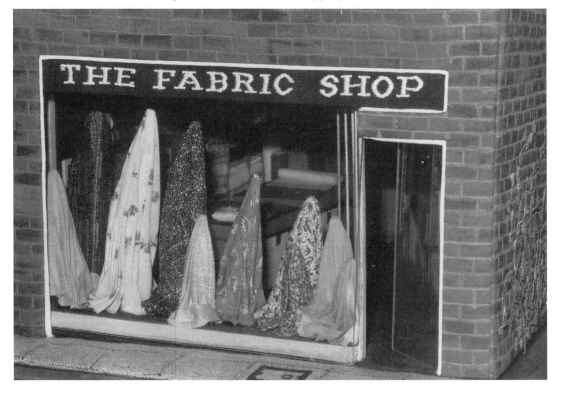

Details of the fabric shop.

thickness of fabrics must be taken into account, so that they do not dominate the final panel too much. Thin card makes a good backing and all the extra pieces should be applied while the background fabric is on a rigid frame.

The other example is the fabric shop embroidered and constructed by Lily Waldron. The entire shop is 25 cm high × 37 cm wide ($9\frac{3}{4}$ × $14\frac{1}{2}$ in.) and 55 cm (22 in.) in depth, making it approximately one-twelfth scale. The miniature embroidery includes: buttons and buckles represented by using a variety of woven wheels in one strand of stranded cotton. Cards of binding, laces, etc. were worked in satin and back stitch, with couching in a variety of threads such as stranded cotton, silk and metallic ones. Excellent use was also made of tiny patterned fabrics for bales in the window and on the shelves, with machine embroidery, patchwork and quilting for much of the exterior detail of the shop.

Suppliers

Names of specific retail shops can be found in *Embroidery*, the magazine published quarterly by The Embroiderers' Guild, Apartment 41, Hampton Court Palace, East Molesey, Surrey KT8 9AU. This magazine also covers a wide range of embroidery topics and news. The Royal School of Needlework, 25 Princes Gate, London SW7 1QE can supply a wide range of books, fabrics and threads.

The following firms will give lists of local stockists on request.

United Kingdom

Appleton Bros Ltd
Church Street
Chiswick, London W4

Coats Domestic Marketing Division
39 Durham Street
Glasgow G41 1BS

DMC UK Distributors
Dunlicraft Ltd
Pullman Road
Wigston
Leicester LE8 2DY

Gütermann-Perivale
Wadsworth Road
Greenford
Middlesex UB6 7JS

Madeira Threads (UK) Ltd
Ryder House
Back Lane
Boroughbridge
North Yorkshire

C.M. Offray and Son Ltd (Ribbons)
Fir Tree Place
Church Road
Ashford
Middlesex TW15 2PH

Paterna Persian Yarn
NeedleArt House
P.O. Box 13
Albion Mills
Wakefield WF2 9SG

USA

Appleton Bros of London
West Main Road
Little Compton
Rhode Island 02837

The DMC Corporation
107 Trumbell Street
Elizabeth
New Jersey 07206

Gütermann of America Inc
501 Archdale Drive
Charlotte
North Carolina 28210-4237

C.M. Offray & Son Inc
Route 24,
PO Box 601
Chester
New Jersey 07930-0601

Specialist suppliers of dollshouse textiles

Val Anderson (dollshouse linen, bedspreads)
58 Highfield Avenue
May Bank
Newcastle-under-Lyme
Staffordshire ST5 0JQ

Carol Black (dollshouse patchwork, also mail order catalogue for
other dollshouse items)
'Sun Hill'
Great Strickland
Penrith
Cumbria CA10 3DF

Jean Brown (dollshouse carpets to commission and kits)
26 St Johns Road
Ludlow
Shropshire

Book list

This is just a selection of the many excellent embroidery books now available through shops and libraries.

General books on embroidery

BUTLER, ANNE. *Batsford Encyclopaedia of Embroidery Stitches* London: Batsford, 1979 (Paperback 1983).

HOWARD, CONSTANCE. *Embroidery and Colour* London: Batsford 1976.

HOWARD, CONSTANCE. *Inspiration for Embroidery* London: Batsford, 1966 (Paperback 1985).

Golden Hands Encyclopaedia of Embroidery London: Collins, 1973.

THOMAS, MARY. *Mary Thomas's Dictionary of Embroidery Stitches* London: Hodder & Stoughton, 1934.

THOMAS, MARY. *Mary Thomas's Embroidery Book* London: Hodder & Stoughton, 1936.

Books on particular techniques

BEANEY, JAN. *Stitches – New Approaches* London: Batsford, 1985.

BEST, MURIEL. *Stumpwork* London: Batsford, 1987.

LEMON, JANE. *Embroidered Boxes* London: Faber & Faber 1980, (Batsford paperback 1984

E. GEDDES & M. MCNEILL. *Blackwork Embroidery* London: Mills & Boon 1965 (Dover Paperback 1976).

MCNEILL, MOYRA. *Pulled Thread* London: Mills & Boon, 1971.

MCNEILL, MOYRA. *Lace and See Through Techniques* London: Batsford, 1985.

NORDFORS, JILL. *Needlelace & Needleweaving* Studio Vista, 1974.

PASCOE, MARGARET. *Blackwork Embroidery* London: Batsford, 1986.

PULS, HERTA. *The Art of Cutwork & Appliqué* London: Batsford, 1978.

RUSSELL, PAT. *Lettering for Embroidery* London: Batsford, 1971.

Books and magazines which include some articles on miniature embroidery

JOHNSON, AUDREY. *Furnishing Dolls Houses* G. Bell and Sons, 1972.

COLEMAN, DOROTHY S., ELIZABETH S. and EVELYN J. *The Collector's Book of Doll Clothes: Costumes in Miniature 1700–1929* New York: Crown Publishers, 1975.

MERRILL, VIRGINIA and JESSOP, JEAN. *Needlework in Miniature* New York: Crown Publishers, 1978.

International Dolls House News (published quarterly). PO Box 79, Southampton, SO9 7EZ.

The Home Miniaturist (published bi-monthly). 18 Calvert Road, Dorking, Surrey RH4 1LS.

Nutshell News (published monthly). Boynton and Associates Inc. Clifton House, Clifton, VA 22024 USA.

General craft magazines

Popular Crafts (published monthly). 1 Golden Square, London WIR 3AB.

McCall's Needlework and Crafts (published monthly). PO Box 10787, Des Moines, Iowa 50349, USA.

Index

Numbers in *italics* refer to pages on which illustrations occur.

Accessories 22–5, 90, 101
Agates 61, 89
Alphabets 55, 56, 57
Animals 50, 51, 71, 73, 84
Architecture 46, 47, 50, 51, 61, 91
Atmosphere, creating an 52–4

Bags and purses 16, 17
Beads 23, 91–2
Bookmarks 92, 60
Boxes 44, 71, 77, 94–5, 98–9

Cards, greetings 30, 31, 32, 48, 49, 56, 97
Christmas decorations 87, 93, 110
Colour 35, 48–9
Constructed fabrics 24

Design
    reduction in size 37–8
    squaring for canvas 64–5
    transferring 59
Dolls cushions 80, 110, 111
Dollshouse items 29, 96
    beds and bedspreads 33, 75, 80, 82, 98
    carpets 66–8
    christening gowns 88
    curtains and cushions 63, 74
    pictures 29, 73, 92
Drawing for design 27, 40–7

Fabrics 18–20, 27, 48–9, 114, 115
    fabric frames 108–10
    water soluble 23, 87
Flowers 15, 17, 30, 46, 74, 85
Frames 54, 102–5
Fruit 41

Gardens 35–6, 50, 83, 96
Geometric designs 16, 40, 52, 61, 62, 74, 85
Glue 20, 25, 97, 110

Historical examples 13–17, 84, 85, 150
Human figures 34, 51, 52

Interfacing 23, 110

Jewellery 28, 87, 92, 93, 110

Kinetic embroidery 94

Lacing over card 105–6

Landscapes 43–5, 50, 66, 73, 104
Lettering 31, 54–7

Maps 72

Needlecases 30, 52, 63, 100, 110
Needles 20, 25–6

Paints and dyes 41
Paper for design 39–40
Photographs 22, 27, 38–9
Pictures, embroidered 14, 23, 30, 44–5, 51, 104
Pincushions 13, 30, 95, 110

Ribbon embroidery 22, 78–83

Samplers 52, 55, 112–14
Sewing machine 86–9, 97–8, 100
Stitches
    couching 48, 73
    Guilloche 21
    ladder 99
    long legged cross 100
    single stitch embroidery 49, 70, 73

Techniques
    appliqué 82, 83–5
    Assisi 69, 111
    blackwork 34, 51, 69, 70, 111
    canvas work 13, 14, 17, 55, 62–8, 84, 85
    couching 71–2
    crewel work 71
    cross stitch 69
    darning 73–4
    fabrics drawn and cut 85–6
    needlelace 89
    net embroidery 73, 74
    patchwork 33, 75–7, 79–83, 95
    quilting 77–8
    raised embroidery and stump work 14, 23, 89–91, 92
    silk embroidery 29, 72–3, 92
    smocking 90, 91
    surface stitchery 15, 36, 57, 70–5, 111
    white work 74
Texture 35, 40
Threads 20–2, 27, 28
Three dimensional 14, 15, 29, 92–6, 115
Trees 87
Two-sided embroidery 92–3, 110–11

Window mounts 107–8